KT-160-426

BFI WORKING PAPERS

CINEMA AND THE REALMS OF ENCHANTMENT

*Lectures, Seminars and Essays by
Marina Warner and Others*

Edited by Duncan Petrie

BFI PUBLISHING

First published in 1993 by the
British Film Institute
21 Stephen Street
London W1P 1PL

The British Film Institute exists to encourage the
development of film, television and video in the United
Kingdom, and to promote knowledge, understanding and
enjoyment of the culture of the moving image. Its activities
include the National Film and Television Archive; the
National Film Theatre; the Museum of the Moving Image;
the London Film Festival; the production and distribution of
film and video; funding and support for regional activities;
Library and Information Services; Stills, Posters and
Designs; Research; Publishing and Education; and the
monthly *Sight and Sound* magazine.

British Library Cataloguing in Publication Data.
A catalogue record for this book is available
from the British Library.

ISBN: 0–85170–405–0 pbk

Cover design by Roger Walton

Typeset in 10 on 11.5pt Sabon by
Rowland Phototypesetting Limited
Bury St Edmunds, Suffolk
and printed in Great Britain by
St Edmundsbury Press Limited
Bury St Edmunds, Suffolk

CONTENTS

BFI WORKING PAPERS

Executive Editor: Colin MacCabe

BFI Working Papers are published twice a year, intended to make theoretical and practical contributions to debate and reflect the wide and eclectic range of research activities and interests undertaken by the BFI. Previous volumes have been tied to a conference and a seminar series respectively. The present volume originates principally from the work of a visiting BFI Research Fellow. Working papers are intended to bring together the writings and ideas of experienced commentators and critics while providing an important opportunity for new talent whenever possible.

Already published:

1. *Screening Europe: Image and Identity in Contemporary European Cinema*

2. *New Questions of British Cinema*

NOTES ON CONTRIBUTORS

Marina Warner was born in London in 1946; her mother is Italian, her father English. She has been writing since she was a student, and has published novels as well as historical studies, mainly of mythology and female symbolism (*Alone of All Her Sex: the Myth and Cult of the Virgin Mary*; *Joan of Arc: the Image of Female Heroism*; *Monuments and Maidens*). She was a Guest Scholar at The Getty Institute for the History of Arts and the Humanities 1987–8; Erasmus University, Rotterdam, made her Tinbergen Professor in 1991, where she gave a series of public lectures on fairy tale. As a Visiting Fellow of the British Film Institute in 1992 she continued her research, and a full study of fairy tale, *From the Beast to the Blonde*, will soon be published. She will be giving the Reith Lectures in 1994, and in the meantime is working on a study of the banana, its cultural and historical significance. Her most recent publications are *Indigo, or Mapping the Waters*, a novel about imperialism in the Caribbean, inspired by *The Tempest*, and a collection of short stories, *The Mermaids in the Basement*.

Rosemary Creeser is director of Wesbourne Film Distribution, specialists in classic children's films. She also combines a career in social research and has published work encompassing girls' education, teenage smoking and children's leisure activities. From an early age she has been fascinated by fairy tales and includes Cocteau's *La Belle et la bête* as one of her most significant inspirations.

Duncan Petrie is research officer at the British Film Institute. He has written *Creativity and Constraint in the British Film Industry*, is the co-editor of *Bill Douglas: A Lanternist's Account*, and has edited two previous volumes of BFI Working Papers – *Screening Europe* and *New Questions of British Cinema*. He is currently writing a history of British cinematography.

Terry Staples is a freelance writer and researcher. He has programmed for children at the National Film Theatre for the last ten years and has organised four International Children's London Film Festivals. He is the author of numerous articles about aspects of children's cinema, and of the *Piccolo Factbook of Film and Video*, published in 1985.

John O. Thompson is MA course director and an education officer at the BFI. His books include *Monty Python: Complete and Utter Theory of the Grotesque*; *Shakespeare, Meaning and Metaphor* (with Ann Thompson); *The Media Reader* (co-edited with Manuel Alvarado); *Contemporary Poetry Meets Modern Literary Theory* (co-edited with Anthony Easthope). He has also written several articles on screen acting.

ACKNOWLEDGMENTS

Thanks are due to the following people for their support, advice and ideas in relation to both Marina Warner's Research Fellowship and this collection:

Robert Carver, Rosemary Creeser, Pete Flower, Roma Gibson, Maggi Hurt, Esther Johnson, Dawn King, Yvonne Salmon, John Smoker, Nicholas Tucker and the BFI staff who attended Marina's seminars.

The film still from *The Singing Ringing Tree* is courtesy of DEFA (Schütt)/PROGRESS Film-Verleih. Thanks also to BFI Stills, Posters and Designs, the National Film and Television Archive and the National Film Theatre.

INTRODUCTION

Duncan Petrie

Like the first two volumes of BFI Working Papers, *Screening Europe* and *New Questions of British Cinema*, this publication arises from recent research activity within the British Film Institute. The centre-piece of this volume is the work of the celebrated scholar and novelist Marina Warner, who was a BFI Visiting Research Fellow in the winter of 1992. During the period of her fellowship, Marina examined the subject of fairy tale and cinema. This research resulted in a season of films at the National Film Theatre, a public lecture to introduce that season, and two other lectures presented to Institute staff and a hand-ful of invited guests, each of which was followed by a lively discussion. These three presentations were so interesting and full of insight that it seemed not only appropriate but necessary to find some way of making them available to a wider public. Hence it was decided that they should form the central theme of the third volume of BFI Working papers.

Consequently, the first half of this volume comprises edited versions of the transcripts of the three lectures. These are transcripts, effectively work in progress, provisional rather than fully polished writings as such, and footnotes are not included. The highlights of the discussions which followed the lectures to BFI staff have been included where appropriate. These serve to extend and clarify the debate, raising sev-eral interesting issues along the way. Wherever possible the individuals making comments or asking questions have been identified. The majority of these are Institute staff but two of the BFI's guests contrib-uted significantly to the discussions: Robert Carver, an independent film-maker, broadcaster and film critic for *The Times Educational Supplement*, and Nicholas Tucker from the Department of Psychology at the University of Sussex.

This material is supplemented by a series of essays, some directly inspired by Marina Warner's lectures at the BFI, which explore certain central issues she raises. Of particular salience are, on the one hand, the considerable influence of fairy tale narrative and motifs on popular cinema, and, on the other, the problematic construction of 'the child'

1

by adults in the context of the production, distribution and exhibition of audiovisual products.

The question of fantasy and its relationship to cinema continues to be of interest to film scholars, providing one of the poles of the realism/fantasy dichotomy which lies at the heart of much theorising about the cinema. This is a reflection of a fundamental aesthetic duality which generated, at the very birth of the medium, two opposing tendencies: one towards the recording or documenting of external 'reality', the other towards the imaginative use of cinematic illusion. These 'tendencies' were explored and developed at roughly the same time in France by Louis Lumière and Georges Méliès respectively.

Unsurprisingly, this duality has greatly influenced writing and thinking about the cinema from the first wave of film theory in the 30s, characterised by 'essentialist' positions on the cinema's true aesthetic vocation, such as those associated with the champion of a realist aesthetic like Siegfried Kracauer[1] on the one hand, and the anti-realist Rudolf Arnheim[2] on the other. The tension between realism and fantasy continued to be a central concern of subsequent generations of theoretical enquiry, informing, as James Donald points out in the Introduction to his own excellent collection of writings, *Fantasy and the Cinema*, much of the agenda-setting *Screen* project of the 70s and early 80s.[3]

These issues continue to delineate a fruitful area of work, with recent considerations of fantasy and horror films (the horror genre has tended to dominate within the broader category of 'fantasy' in film studies), opening up more sophisticated and challenging insights into such questions as the nature of cinematic spectacle, the construction of gendered subjects in the text and the psychic processes of identification.[4] As Donald suggests, the revival of interest in fantasy is related to the belief that fantasy helps to explain the fascination, and so the power, of cinema. It also offers a way of thinking about what he refers to as the 'complex interaction marked by both the dynamics of the psychic and the social'[5] – that is to say, the relationship between internal subjective factors and external objective conditions within the realm of the cinematic experience.

Taken collectively, the three contributions by Marina Warner to this volume forcefully address this 'complex interaction', but in a rather different way from orthodox film scholarship. Warner's acute sensitivity to history, the changing role of story-telling in society, and the transformations which have occurred in terms of discourse and meaning, make her arguments both compelling and perceptive. One tends to forget that the history of cinema is relatively short and that the modes of narration and codes of representation which distinguish the medium are prefigured by a vast and extensive history of cultural production and transmission which have been highly influential on the new medium.

In 'The Uses of Enchantment', Warner immediately identifies the close primary relationship between cinema and fantasy I allude to above. But she understands that the on-screen magic tricks of Georges Méliès and other pioneers emerge from not only a vaudeville tradition of conjuring but also the realm of the fantastic in pre-cinema optical entertainments such as the phantasmagoria, shadow plays and magic lantern shows. It was absolutely appropriate that the new medium, with its technological potential for illusion and optical trickery, should build upon and expand the scope of such forms of popular entertainment.

Within this context of early cinema, Warner focuses on the connections between the cinema and the world of fairy tales. This affinity goes beyond the realm of mere magic, as she pointed out in the programme notes which accompanied her season of films at the National Film Theatre:

the camera acts as an anonymous narrator, in the same way as the storyteller, and much of its material is popular: as a medium, cinema desires the audience's pleasure and consciously observes its possible constituency, its taste and interests, as a storyteller in the bazaar responds to the audience, as Scheherazade made sure she was pleasing the Sultan.[6]

Fairy tales are fundamentally embedded in popular culture, being rooted in an oral folk tradition and passed down from generation to generation. These stories were later collected and enshrined in print by people like Charles Perrault, the Brothers Grimm and Hans Christian Andersen, whose names have become synonymous with the fairy tale tradition. This process often involved the re-editing of tales on the basis that versions in circulation were often explicitly violent or sexual in nature. It also entailed a conception of the appropriateness of fairy tales to the Victorian bourgeois project of moral education and consequently the identification of the child as primary audience. Thus a crucial consideration in the analysis of fairy tales, in the various realms of oral, literary and cinematic transmission, is to ascertain who is telling the tale, who is the tale being told to, and what is at stake in this interaction. The process of storytelling is never neutral, there are always wider considerations of a social and ideological nature, particularly when we are talking about a kind of narrative tradition which has been so enduring in its popularity, has embraced different modes of

3

transformation, and which has been regarded by various critics as both profoundly Utopian and insidiously reactionary in its effects.

Central to any academic consideration of the fairy tale tradition is the question of their interpretation. Warner alludes to the numerous interpretations of the fairy tale, some of which stress the relationship of such tales to universal psychic processes, others to historically changing material circumstances. What underpins many of them, however, is the idea that fairy tales contain some instruction, some mechanism for helping us to understand and cope with the problems of everyday life. This dimension, when elided with a consideration of changing value systems and social mores, helps us to understand the motives of those who have worked in both the transmission and interpretation of fairy tales, from Perrault and the Grimms through to more contemporary figures like Bruno Bettelheim and Angela Carter.

Of course, such individuals often have very different perspectives and projects. To take some more recent examples: Bettelheim argues that fairy tales characteristically state an existential dilemma in an uncomplicated, clear-cut manner, which permits children to confront and grasp the underlying meanings of these conflicts in their most essential form, enabling them to work through the conflicts and experiences in their own lives which otherwise would be repressed and perhaps cause psychological disturbance.[7] On the other hand, some critics of Bettelheim take him to task for failing to comprehend the destructive messages in fairy tales (which reinforce patriarchal social relations), but nevertheless endorse the positive aspects of the appropriation of symbolic meanings by children, albeit with a keener sense of social stratification and power structures.[8] Angela Carter's reinterpretation of classic fairy tales, *The Bloody Chamber*, seeks to provide a feminist corrective to the patriarchal sanitisation of these stories. Consequently, her versions of *Bluebeard*, *Red Riding Hood* and other familiar tales seek to re-establish female sexuality as something other than a passive adjunct to male requirements and to restore mother–daughter relationships as a positive force.[9]

Warner, who has a great deal of affinity with Carter's position, also takes Bettelheim to task for his failure to consider the influence of material circumstances on the generation of fairy tales. She, too, is extremely critical of certain versions of classic tales, both written and filmed. Indeed, within the complex historical web of interpretation and meaning, Warner identifies a development described as 'a regressive shift away from a literature and a cinema of imaginative resistance towards one of social adaptation and compliance'. In a 1992 article, for example, she criticises Disney for adaptations of classic fairy tales like *Snow White* and *Cinderella* which hold up 'simpering, gutless, niminy-piminy idiots as paragons and introduced children everywhere

4

to expect malignancy from older women'.[10] Such a position would seem to be echoed by the arguments of Jack Zipes who writes:

From the very beginning folk tales tended to be contradictory, containing Utopian and conservative elements. What kept the Utopian aspect alive was the context in which the tales were actively received and retold by the common people. . . . Today the audience for fairy tales, whether they be transmitted as a literary text, film, play, advertisement, or TV show, has become passive, and the narrative perspective and voice are generally guided by commercial interests.[11]

For Zipes it is the appropriation and subsequent commodification of the tales by capitalism which have destroyed their progressive elements. Warner, however, takes more of a feminist than a Marxist approach, believing that despite the general historical trend there are exceptions to the rule, which she proceeds to identify. As she explained in her NFT programme notes:

for this season I've chosen some movies which I hope reveal a different side of fairy tale on film: its capacity to face up to real-life difficulties and deal with them imaginatively, to make the best of adversity. If a popular medium can't challenge the *status quo* as well as support it, we might as well shrug our way into an early grave.[12]

Central to Warner's project of reclaiming some progressive impulse in the cinematic rendering of fairy tale narrative is a consideration of its relationship to female experience and, particularly, to rites of passage. Consequently, several of the films considered in 'The Uses of Enchantment', such as *The Company of Wolves* (1984), *The Wizard of Oz* (1925), *La Fille de l'eau* (1924), *L'Atalante* (1934), *Peau d'âne* (1971) and *Die Marquise von O* (1976) feature female protagonists who have to encounter and deal with dramatic and fundamental changes in their lives. These changes are related to the transformation of girls into women: the onset of puberty, emergence of adult sexuality, the change in social status from daughters to wives, with all the excitements and dangers this entails. In other words, the integration of psycho-sexual and social transformations'. What these films offer is a progressive understanding of the very real problems and dilemmas women have had to face, and cope with. They also feature strong, feisty female characters, far removed from the passive simpering heroines of the Disney versions of the fairy tale classics such as *Snow White*, *Sleeping Beauty* and *Cinderella*.

5

What is also interesting about Warner's selection of films is that none of the titles she invokes could be considered a film specifically for children (indeed, only one of the feature films in the selection of twelve in her season falls into that category – *The Singing Ringing Tree*, which I shall consider below). But the best-known versions of fairy tales in literature (the collections of the Grimms and Andersen, the *Ladybird* books of my own childhood in the 60s) and the cinema (Disney) do explicitly address the child as implied audience. This begs a whole set of questions regarding the moral and didactic agendas of the teller, which will be raised again below in Terry Staples' essay.

In 'Through a Child's Eyes', Warner considers another way in which the child figures within the process of the production and transmission of fairy tale narrative in cinema by examining films which are not necessarily made for children but which feature a child as narrator. By constructing a cinematic viewpoint approximating that of the child, film-makers obviously bring into play certain assumption and preconceptions about the nature of childhood. This frequently involves the prelapsarian notion of innocence and the implication that children, by virtue of not being bound by adult rationality, have greater access to the world of imagination and fantasy. However, as Warner points out, this serves the purpose of displacing adult irrationality and fears on to children: behind the child narrator lurks the adult.

This whole question of 'the impossible relation between adult and child' is explored by Jacqueline Rose in the context of children's literary fiction, and in particular J. M. Barrie's *Peter Pan*.[13] Rose is interested not so much in the needs of the child but what lies behind the adult constructions of 'the child'. A crucial consideration is the implications behind an adult masking of child sexuality:

> Freud is known to have undermined the concept of childhood innocence, but his real challenge is easily lost if we see in the child merely a miniature of what our sexuality eventually comes to be. The child is sexual, but its sexuality (bisexual, polymorphous, perverse) threatens our own at its very roots. Setting up the child as innocent is not, therefore, repressing its sexuality – it is above all holding off any possible challenge to our own.[14]

But, as Rose points out, it is not only sexuality which is denied. By positing a transcendent notion of childhood or the 'eternal child', we deny any interrogation of the category 'child' and fail to locate this category within material social structures, which suppresses questions of division and difference, be it class, culture or literacy. Indeed, such divisions effectively undermine any generalised concept of the child.

Consequently, for Rose, the glorification of the child goes hand in hand with the masking of questions of sexuality and materialism. This statement is in relation here to a specific literary text (*Peter Pan*) but has implications for children's fiction, and cinema in general. Rose writes: 'This suggests not only a refusal to acknowledge difficulties and contradictions in relation to childhood; it implies that we *use* the image of the child to deny those same difficulties in relation to ourselves.'[15] It is therefore misleading to think about the meaning of fairy tales and the dynamics of narrative construction and transmission without considering this intriguing and problematic relation between adult and child. I shall return to this question below.

In developing the depth of her analysis of the fairy tale tradition, Warner considers one of the earliest fairy tales – the story of *Cupid and Psyche* – dating back to the second century AD, to indicate the classical roots of many of the key themes in the fairy tale tradition. These include issues such as the danger of looking love in the face, which lies behind the *Beauty and the Beast* tales; the perils of female curiosity, which echoes in other formative stories such as that of Eve and Pandora; the idea of innocent, child-like heroines. As Warner demonstrates, the question of gender is frequently aligned with innocence and, while the arrival of a sexed identity spells the end of a certain kind of innocence, the pre-pubescent child, whether a boy or a girl, is often given a feminine inflection.

The theme of gender and fantasy is further explored in Warner's third contribution, 'Women against Women in the Old Wives' Tale', which begins by considering another key theme in fantasy film and literature: the creation of human life. While the most familiar version of this in the cinema is the Frankenstein story, this is atypical of the tradition in general in that the creation is male. More often than not we are dealing with female automata: artificial women fashioned by men as idealised versions of womankind, which again echoes the creation of Eve and Pandora. Examples from the cinema examined by Warner include Lubistch's *Die Puppe* (1919) and James Whale's *Bride of Frankenstein* (1935). The creation of woman often involves some kind of fall – frequently the direct result of female curiosity, a failure to obey the instructions of her creator.

If the danger represented by the figure of the beast is a lack of understanding of the primal force of emergent sexuality, then the only way this can be overcome or civilised (transformed from hideous beast to handsome prince) is through the pursuit of knowledge. This entails a process of transmission which in preliterate society (the context of oral storytelling) is dependent on the faculty of speech. However, when such acts are perpetrated by women they are often regarded at best as idle or worthless activity (the derogatory implications behind the phrase 'old wives' tale') but more often as dangerous. This leads Warner to consider the history of misogyny in relation to female speech and female curiosity, tracing examples from medieval writings and representations, through the fairy tale tradition in literature and cinema. The popular image of storytelling round the hearth often involves misogynistic representations of the old crone as the teller. Furthermore, within the stories themselves, particularly the sanitised versions in print and their cinematic offspring, you have the figures of the witch and the wicked stepmother who are either ugly or garrulous, or both, contrasted with the heroines who have youth, beauty, and a certain verbal reticence to commend them.

The contributions by John Thompson, on *Cat People* (1942) and *The Curse of the Cat People* (1944), and myself, on *Batman Returns* (1992), are attempts to further demonstrate the applicability of some of the key issues raised by Marina Warner when applied to the interpretation of specific filmic texts. What these essays share is an interest in beastly transformation, as a motif for emergent sexuality, and in particular female sexuality. Where they deviate from the classical version of *Beauty and the Beast* is that the beast is female rather than male, and consequently not set up as something external which the heroine must confront and come to terms with. These beasts are internal and involve a very different kind of psychic struggle. Moreover, the beast is represented not by the figure of the bear, wolf or wild boar as in cinematic versions of the traditional story, but rather by the figure of the cat, that most feminine of animals.

Val Lewton's first *Cat People* film tells the story of Irena, a Serbian refugee who believes that she is a member of a race of cat people and that sexual contact will cause her to turn into a panther. Unsurprisingly, her frigidity gives her husband cause for concern and he sends her to a psychiatrist. Lewton established a reputation as a producer of low-budget horror films for RKO in the 40s which eschewed the usual visual shocks and monsters for a more subtle, suggestive style rooted in film noir lighting and atmosphere. He worked with three directors on eight features over a period of four years – Jacques Tourneur, Mark Robson and Robert Wise. Tourneur was responsible for *Cat People* and Wise for *Curse of the Cat People*, the only sequel in the Lewton canon.

The contemplation of female sexuality in *Cat People* is almost totally negative. Irena is doubly cursed in that it is not only sexual passion which can turn her into a beast but also sexual jealousy. Caught in this double bind she is unable either to have sexual relations with her husband or cope with any attraction he might have for another woman. In the end this predicament can only destroy her and the film ends with her inevitable destruction. However, in *The Curse*

8

of the Cat People, Irena returns as a spiritual presence to comfort the lonely daughter of her ex-husband and his second wife. She is dressed like a fairy tale princess and assumes an aura of 'innocence' – in part, the projection of the innocent child who is scolded by her father for her flights of fantasy. In this way the film embraces fantasy as positive, but firmly locates such fantasies within childhood. Yet if it also serves to 'repair' the first text, as John Thompson suggests, it does so by reducing Irena from sexual being to prelapsarian innocent. The refusal to deal with sexuality in *Curse of the Cat People* (particularly in the light of the previous film) represents a major retreat, echoing the kind of processes unmasked by Rose in relation to *Peter Pan*.

Seen from a 90s perspective, *Batman Returns* is a much more post-feminist text in its contemplation of female sexuality. What is particularly interesting is the way in which Selina Kyle, the catwoman, is set up as a version of the archetypal fairy tale princess, rejects the traditional role which is offered to her and instead decides, against the odds, to preserve her new-found independence and self-reliance. The metaphorical unleashing of her sexuality (when she is first transformed into a cat) comes as a direct result of having been punished for her curiosity ('Don't you know what curiosity did to the cat?' asks the sinister Max Shreck before pushing Selina through the window to her (supposed) death several flights below in the street); despite the difficulties she experiences in controlling her new powers, she refuses to be subjugated to the interests and desires of the men in the film.

Batman Returns is also interesting in the way it brings another literary tradition, adopted by the cinema, to bear on the fairy tale narrative – the idea of the double or *doppelgänger*, whose literary origins lie in the romantic tradition. The idea of the beast entails a conception of a human subject at war with itself, unable to control or reconcile different urges or drives. Indeed, the romantics' decentring of the unified utilitarian subject provided the groundwork for the later emergence of psychoanalysis, with its model of the divided psyche and the tensions generated between ego, id and super ego. As I attempt to argue, *Batman Returns*, in addition to its many filmic references, is also knowing in its borrowings from Freudian psychoanalysis, albeit in a rather simplistic way.

The theme of transformation figures strongly in *The Singing Ringing Tree*, produced in what was East Germany in the 50s and one of the films chosen by Marina Warner in her NFT season. As Rosemary Creeser points out, unlike the majority of fairy tales, in this case both the princess and the prince undergo transformations. The princess who is beautiful but vain and self-centred becomes ugly (the idea that beauty is only skin deep) and has to learn to love others in order to restore her physical beauty. The prince, who is in love with the princess

9

but has been spurned by her, is transformed into a bear by the wicked dwarf and it requires her true love (à la *Beauty and the Beast*) to change him back into a man. In this way *The Singing Ringing Tree* is both a moral tale and, secondarily, a meditation on awakening sexuality.

Creeser then recounts how and why she decided to acquire the film and put it into distribution in the UK (twenty-five years after it had been screened on British television), before going on to briefly consider the reactions of both adults (who had seen the film on television during their childhood, as indeed I did) and children. What is striking is the power that the images, and the fantasy world conjured up in the process, hold for both groups despite a certain lack of visual sophistication on the part of the film when compared with contemporary high-tech special effects productions. What Creeser demonstrates is the broad appeal of cinematic fantasy: films such as *The Singing Ringing Tree* obviously work for adults as well as for children despite being constructed specifically as entertainment for the latter group. This brings us back to the thorny question of adult fantasy and constructions of the 'child'.

The Singing Ringing Tree was premièred at the 1990 Junior London Film Festival, programmed by Terry Staples whose own contribution to this volume traces the various initiatives in Britain to provide a specialist cinema for children (as distinct from a cinema for adults or family audiences). He focuses on the period from 1929 (the point which saw the introduction of sound) up to 1950 and his title 'Doing them Good' encapsulates the philanthropic sense of moral or public duty which underpinned several of these initiatives. We are back on the terrain of the adult–child relationship and the construction of the latter in relation to cultural products which are construed to have some beneficial effects.

Staples examines the interventions of Sidney Bernstein, owner of the Granada chain of cinemas in the 20s and 30s, and then of J. Arthur Rank in the 40s. Both initiatives were inspired by a mixture of philanthropy and commercial speculation – both Bernstein and Rank believed that specialised cinema for children could be both a morally beneficial and a profitable enterprise. There is an important distinction between these operations, however. Bernstein believed that some films were simply not suitable for children and that there was a need to consider the provision of films for children in the way one would consider the need for children's literature. His solution was to programme films which, although not necessarily made for children, were nevertheless considered to be suitable. The notion of 'suitability' seems to have been embodied by films which had a clear moral message or were 'harmless entertainment'.

10

This policy of 'doing them no harm' shifts to a project of actively 'doing them good' with the involvement of Rank, who was a strong Methodist. While Bernstein concentrated on exhibition, Rank, who had the benefit of a vertically integrated film combine at his disposal, was able to produce the films he wanted to show in his cinemas. He subsequently set up a unit, Children's Entertainment Films, to produce films specifically for children which would embody the kind of morality deemed appropriate and beneficial to them. Staples discusses how and why certain parameters of suitability were defined as CEF became an established producer of children's cinema.

One interesting aesthetic shift during this period was a move away from fantasy to realism. As Staples points out, prior to Rank's involvement in the production of children's cinema, fantasy films imported from the Soviet Union (an early echo of *The Singing Ringing Tree*?) were popular with audiences who attended the Saturday matinées screened by the Odeon circuit (incidentally, owned by Rank). By contrast, the standard CEF product usually utilised a contemporary realist mode, an emphasis not out of step with what was considered 'quality' British cinema by critics, as John Ellis has shown.[16] Such a strategy embraces the basic initiative to produce morality tales (which the Soviet fairy tales had also been) but in this case by foregrounding 'knowable' characters in 'knowable' situations.

The desires of Bernstein, and particularly Rank, to 'do them good' has echoes in the field of literature. The kind of book considered to do the child most good is characterised by Jacqueline Rose as 'the book which secures the reader to its intent and can be absolutely sure of its effects'.[17] In the context of cinema, just as in literature, the adult figures as the producer of a text with the child cast as receiver, but neither enter the space in between. The adult may construct an image of the child within the text but, as Rose argues, this is done in order to secure the child who is outside the text – 'the one who does not come so easily within its grasp'. Children's fiction and cinema necessarily sets up the child as an outsider to its own process. The agenda is consequently always that of the adult. In this way, one could argue for the impossibility of children's cinema as Rose argues for the impossibility of children's fiction. The evidence would seem to support this in that many children, particularly those in their early teens, seem to prefer watching films which are not especially designated as children's films.

Notes

1. See, for example, Kracauer's *From Caligari to Hitler* (London: Dennis Dobson, 1947), a study of German cinema from 1919 to 1933 (the

11

Expressionist period) which he criticises for neglecting to consider directly the political upheavals in Germany by favouring fantasy and being dedicated to formalism; this actually helped to pave the way for Hitler's rise by subtly diverting the audience from a serious appraisal of social realities.

2. Arnheim's *Film as Art* (London: Faber & Faber, 1958) is a statement of the anti-realist tradition. For Arnheim, if cinema were the mere mechanical reproduction of real life then it would deny it the status of art, which is precisely what he wants to assert.
3. James Donald, general introduction to the anthology *Fantasy and the Cinema*, Donald (ed.) (London: BFI, 1989).
4. This includes Donald's collection and Carol J. Clover's *Men, Women and Chainsaws* (London: BFI, 1992).
5. Donald, *Fantasy and the Cinema*, p. 6.
6. Marina Warner, 'Fairy tale and Film: the uses of enchantment', NFT Booklet, February 1992, p. 2.
7. Bruno Bettelheim, *The Uses of Enchantment: The Meaning and Importance of Fairy Tales* (London: Peregrine Books, 1978), Introduction.
8. Caroline Steedman, 'The Tidy House of Fiction: Sex Stories, Gender and Language', in *The Tidy House: Little Girls Writing* (London: Virago, 1982).
9. Angela Carter, *The Bloody Chamber* (London: Penguin, 1979). This collection has inspired at least two film adaptations: Neil Jordan's feature film *The Company of Wolves* (1984), co-scripted by Carter, and *The Bloody Chamber* (1984), a thirty-minute short directed by Nick Lewin.
10. Marina Warner, 'Beauty and the Beast', *Sight and Sound*, October 1992.
11. Jack Zipes, *Breaking the Magic Spell* (London: Heinemann, 1979), p. 123.
12. Marina Warner, 'Fairy tale and Film', NFT Booklet, February 1992, p. 3.
13. Jacqueline Rose, *The Case of 'Peter Pan': Or, the Impossibility of Children's Fiction* (London: Macmillan, 1984).
14. Ibid., p. 4.
15. Ibid., p. 8.
16. John Ellis, 'Art, Culture and Quality: Terms for a Cinema in the Forties and Seventies', *Screen*, Autumn 1978.
17. Rose, *The Case of 'Peter Pan'*.

THE USES OF ENCHANTMENT

Lecture at the National Film Theatre, 7 February 1992

Marina Warner

INTRODUCTION BY COLIN MACCABE
It gives me great pleasure to welcome Marina Warner as a Visiting Fellow to the Institute. Marina is the sixth such Fellow, and she is, as I think and hope each one of them has been, a genuine intellectual. Unfortunately, ideas today normally circulate almost entirely within a university context in which the drily scholastic and irrelevantly political rival each other in their inconsequentiality to the study and understanding of the world. What Marina's work over the last twenty years has done is to bring real painstaking historical and academic skills to bear on genuine problems and genuine ways of thinking about the situations we live in. This work has centred on images and representations of the feminine and femininity, and includes major studies of Joan of Arc and the Virgin Mary. More recently, her work has widened to include the topic of childhood and the ways in which we conceive and think of the child. I imagine that her lecture today will somehow embrace both of those concerns.

The reason why Marina is such an appropriate Visiting Fellow is that her work has always been cross-media, cross-cultural, cross-disciplinary. That is to say, she has refused the normal academic divisions of 'literature', 'art history' or whatever, in order to follow themes and representations across cultures (both temporally and spatially) and different media. I am particularly pleased that she has widened her concern with the image to directly address film. Yet it is typical of Marina that, in doing that, she has turned her attention from the most modern form to perhaps the oldest form of narrative we have – the fairy tale. So I would like you to welcome Marina Warner.

THE USES OF ENCHANTMENT
Thank you very much. I must say I really appreciate being invited by the BFI to be a Visiting Fellow. It was a great surprise and so far it's

been a tremendous pleasure because I've been able to watch all these wonderful films which I had never seen before and which I am going to talk about today.

I

When showmen staged the first moving pictures, with zoetropes and other contrivances, the relationship of this new invention to fantasy (as opposed to reality) seemed its most marvellous property. One entertainer at the turn of the century advertised his wares by saying:

> This is a spectacle which man can use to instruct himself in the bizarre effects of the imagination, where it combines vigour and arrangement: I speak of the terror inspired by the shadows, spirits and spells and the occult work of the magician.

The still camera was concurrently busy making an inventory of the world, turning motion, emotion and madness into visual documents, as in the work of Charcot and Muybridge. But the new, *moving* flux of images held out the enthralling possibility of passing beyond the visible to the (normally) invisible, from the real to the supernatural. What is interesting is how often the supernatural was understood to be subjective – produced by the imagination – and how the communication of internal fantasy became one of the central enterprises of the new 'movies'.

Magic and magical tricks became a vehicle for this expression of fantasy. Audiences entertained by goblins, wizards, puffs of smoke, appearances and vanishings, and explosions, did not believe in such manifestations – even if they did believe in some aspects of the world beyond. But the narratives which these effects propelled along met their desires and their hopes.

Georges Méliès, the most brilliant and comic innovator of this kind of early fantasy cinema, was, in his poverty-stricken old age, presented with the *Légion d'Honneur* by Lumière (who by contrast had pioneered the documentary approach to film-making). Lumière told him: 'I salute in you the creator of the cinematographic spectacle.' Working at the turn of the century, when cinema was very much in its infancy, Méliès involved himself in every aspect of the film-making process. He designed costumes and sets, wrote scripts, shot the films, and did the all-important editing for what he described as 'the apotheosis': the final display of visual transformations of great effect. He also acted in his effervescent short films of favourite fairy tales, and his favourite roles are often impish: devils, hobgoblins and the like.

Méliès adapted several fairy stories of Charles Perrault, which had been popular in France since they were first published at the end of the 17th century. He made three different *Cinderellas*, including one in which he plays the clock that strikes midnight. He also made a version of *Peau d'âne (Donkey Skin)*, which I've unfortunately never seen (there's no copy as yet in the National Film Archive), a *Bluebeard*, which features a comic horror image of his wives 'hanging up to dry' in the forbidden room like a macabre washing line or a butcher's cold store, and also a version, currently missing, of *Red Riding Hood*.

Méliès was influenced by the illustrated volumes of stories which were beginning to appear in the second half of the 19th century. These were often splendid illuminated or engraved editions, sometimes in colour which, of course, the earlier movies were not, though he himself hand-tinted some of his frames. The musical theatre of the time also had a bearing on his staging of action – the tableau-like unfolding of the story under a proscenium arch, as it were. The magical effects and visual tricks of Méliès's cinema approximate to the conjuring and fairy lore of the traditional tale. It was Perrault, for instance, who in *Cinderella* added the pumpkin carriage, the rat coachman and the lizard footman to the familiar oral tale of a wronged orphan girl.

In the climactic moments of Méliès's exceptionally high-spirited *Bluebeard*, made in 1901, Bluebeard's most recent wife, his eighth, having seen what lies in wait for her when she uses the forbidden key to enter the bloody chamber, has just run away from him to the top

Peau d'âne (Jacques Demy, 1970)

of the high tower. She beseeches her sister Anne to call for help. Anne is watching from the turret for the brothers who will gallop to her rescue in the nick of time. While she gesticulates frantically, Bluebeard rushes up the spiral stairs to the turret, erupts on to the platform (he's depicted as a hairy foreigner; indeed, there are often traces of the 'Oriental' in traditional depictions of this ogre) and he seizes her by the hair and begins to thrash down the stairs with her bouncing horribly on the steps (the substitution of a dummy here rather adds to the effect of his heedless violence). But her brothers arrive, in the nick of time, and run Bluebeard through with a sword, pinning him against the castle wall. A friendly sprite (Méliès himself) dances on, and in a puff of smoke, conjures all the former wives back to life; they reappear, smiling and well, and looking a bit crowded on Méliès's small stage; then, almost immediately – the speed of Méliès's action gives his wit its great *élan* – eight bridegrooms arrive and claim each of the wives before walking out of shot in a merry bridal procession, while Bluebeard, still pinned to the wall, kicks his legs in comic rage.

But the uses of enchantment in film by no means end with the brilliant French entertainer's high-spirited and absurdist conjuring tricks. Film-makers utilised the medium to pass through outer forms in order to reproduce fantasy in visible, almost palpable, terms. They explored film's unprecedented power to conjure up the inner workings of the mind. Following in the footsteps of the literary form, film from the very beginning explored the territory of fear, showing heroes and heroines dealing with the products of their darkest imaginings. These early works are the precursors of contemporary horror cinema, including slasher movies.

In these two respects – the interest in the imagination and the confrontation of private but universal terrors – film as a genre bears a close affinity with the most popular branch of literary romance. This has been helpfully labelled the 'Wonder Tale' by some critics, or is also sometimes known as the 'Folk Fairy Tale'. (One of the problems with the fairy tale is that very often there aren't any fairies in it, so the use of 'fairy' tale as a genre concept is actually rather misleading; hence the title 'Wonder Tale' is probably more helpful, although it's not a term I usually use.) I'm going to try here to develop this relationship more fully and show how the history of the reception of written fairy stories has been recapitulated to some extent in the development of kindred narratives in the movies.

Fairy tales have been interpreted in innumerable ways. For some (mainly 19th-century) commentators they were the decayed myths of paganism. Cinderella was a goddess whose new-won radiance proclaimed the beginning of spring. For allegorists of a Neo-Platonist turn of mind, fairy tales were scriptures of the spirit, recording universal themes of love and death. For instance, the tale of *Cupid and Psyche* (one of the earliest we have, from Apuleius' second-century metaphysical comic romance *The Golden Ass*) told an eternal story about the loss and recovery of identity through love. Psychoanalysts, beginning with Freud, have continued this line of argument, finding in worldwide folklore the encoded revelations of desire – a symbolic map of the soul/psyche alongside dreams. In the writing of Bruno Bettelheim, Cinderella's slipper becomes a symbol of her sexuality, which, on reaching maturity, she makes over to the prince's care. More recently, the American poet Robert Bly, in his Jungian reading of the Grimms' fairy tale *Iron John*, has produced a blueprint for masculinity: for reactivating the Inner Warrior, the King Within, which entails the end of the wimp, the soft boy, too shell-shocked by mother or the Vietnam War to act as a man.

In counterbalance to these universalising interpretations, a socio-historical school – rather pragmatic, rather earthbound – has emerged which is interested in fairy tales as a more direct impression of reality, a form of popular culture which keeps the memory of actual circumstances (economic, familial, emotional), as well as transforming them in the light of new developments. The fairy tale, subjected to this approach, becomes a tool for thought, a multicoloured skein of images with which to think about the real, both reiterating and shaping the real in restructured narratives, reassembled images.

What is common to both approaches is an acceptance that the fairy tale contains instruction of some sort, and that the stories cannot be seen as purposeless entertainments. This premise allows the interpreters to winkle out their own meanings in order to press the tale into doing service to their own viewpoint. I must confess that I'm probably guilty of that too – we are all interpreters. Nobody denies the potency of these tales, nobody pretends that they do not spell dangers as well as pleasures. In the fields of psychiatry, pedagogy and cultural criticism, the wonder tale is a well-fought terrain and the controversies are by no means settled.

One of the questions that immediately springs to mind as I face this Babel of interpretations is: '*Who* is telling the story?' There quickly follows from that a supplementary question: 'For whom are they telling it?' Both these questions can also be asked of film, of course, and they usually are. Indeed, film, with its habit of taking and reworking well-known stories, helps to point up similar interweaving and retexturing in the verbal story-telling tradition, as the pattern adapts itself to a new warp (the time, the place) and a new weft (the public).

A quick survey reveals an oddly parallel movement in both forms, away from a local oral literature and cinema of imaginative resistance, towards a literature and cinema of social adaptation and even com-

17

pliance. There are exceptions, of course, such as *Celia*, which I shall be discussing in due course. The appearance of a film like *Celia*, written and directed by Ann Turner in Australia (and consequently partly independent of the male boardroom demands for rewrites) coincides with the exhilarating revisionism of the traditional fairy tale in the writings of women like Angela Carter, Ursula LeGuin and Suniti Namjoshi. The teller's enterprise is vital. D. H. Lawrence was right when he said: 'Trust the tale, not the teller,' but only in the sense that the teller is always up to something. The tale sometimes conceals the teller very well and sometimes reveals her or him. In my view, the circumstances in which the tale is told forms another crucial part of the story, too. The interpretive context adds an all-important layer. We are, for instance, all post-Freudian now. Even the dunderhead Prince Charming will be expecting Cinderella to have penis envy!

In *The Uses of Enchantment*, his influential study of fairy tale published in 1976, the psychoanalyst Bruno Bettelheim formulated an interpretation about the place of such stories in children's development which has gained almost canonical status. Bettelheim argued that fairy tales were good for children because they led them to confront their own hostilities, fears and vulnerability. Fairy tales helped them to survive the antagonisms and sufferings in their own lives by showing them their own subjective experiences of life, magnified and intensified, in the plots and figures of the stories: the wicked stepmothers, abandoning fathers, rival siblings and murderous spouses of fairy tales. Bettelheim wrote:

> Those who outlawed traditional folk fairy tales decided that if there were any monsters in fairy tales they must all be friendly. But they missed the monsters a child knows best and is most concerned with: the monster he feels or fears himself to be and which also sometimes persecutes him.

For Bettelheim, the beast lay within, and through fantasy the child could exorcise it or tame it or deal with it otherwise. He spoke enthusiastically, therefore, of such a tale as the Grimm brothers' *The Boy who Set Out to Discover Fear*, otherwise known as *The One who Wanted to Learn How to Shudder*. In the Grimms' story, the hero cannot experience fear. He spends a night under a gibbet and isn't frightened at the corpses hanging above him. He subsequently enters a spellbound castle and confronts fearful monsters.

The story was adapted as a puppet film in Germany in 1935. The film-maker Paul Dihe relished the coincidence of movie magic with the macabre and supernatural and how the potential of animation and special effects lent themselves to the conjuring of a creepy, grisly

18

and exciting world beyond. His images follow the Grimms' story very closely. The young hero laments to himself 'Ah, if I could but shudder!' Suddenly, something cries from the corner, 'Au miau, how cold we are!' The boy replies, 'You fools! What are you crying about? If you are cold, come and take a seat by the fire and warm yourselves.' At that moment two great, bristling black cats appear with one tremendous leap and sit down, one on each side of him, staring savagely with their fiery eyes. 'Comrade, shall we have a game of cards?' they ask, to which the hero replies, 'Why not? . . . What long nails you have, I must first cut them for you.' Thereupon he seizes them by their throats, places them on the cutting board and screws their feet fast. 'My fancy for playing cards has gone,' he remarks before striking them dead and throwing them out into the moat.

After the hero has overwhelmed all the fiends – in grotesque sport with various ghouls, such as playing nine-pins with skulls for balls and bones for pins – he is able at last to reach the treasure in the enchanted castle and win the princess. And it's only in bed with her at the end that he learns how to shudder – when she tips over him a bucket of live fish.

Bettelheim, the good Freudian, concentrates on the sexual overtones of the story, and certainly the image of wriggling fish doesn't appear for the first or last time as a metaphor for erotic discovery – one thinks, for example, of Lorca's line: 'Her thighs slipped from me like startled fishes.' Bettelheim comments that the hero's sexual anxiety froze his earlier responses, making him incapable of pleasure, whose sign is shivering. The monsters here are fantasies, arising from his repugnance of sex and sexuality which prevents him from reaching out to know the shudder of orgasm.

Even though Bettelheim himself was born in Germany and had survived the Nazi years, including internment in a concentration camp, he underestimates the power of fantasy to make and unmake enemies, to raise bogeys of a dangerous order. For I'm going to introduce an unsettling piece of history which offers a context for the film adaptation of *The One who Wanted to Learn How to Shudder* and will alter the effect the film has on you, I believe.

Hitler loved fairy tales. He saw them as the authentic voice of the *Volk* (the folk, the people), and he admired the toughness and cunning which the heroes showed. (Of course, the idea of these tales being pure-grown German was historically completely fraudulent.) This puppet film, made, remember, in 1935, with its tow-headed hero who does not flinch at hideous acts, takes on a rather disturbing character in this context. The physiognomies of the evil spirits and monsters which he dispatches become particularly unsettling when one remembers the Nazi pogroms against Gypsies, gays and, of course, the Jews and all non-Aryans. It's interesting that in the Grimms' story the monsters are actually named as black cats and black dogs, so the appearance in the film of other creatures as well, with grotesque human physiognomies, is a significant change.

When de-Nazification began in Germany after the war, claims of Nordic superiority and suchlike in circulating materials like textbooks were removed. It was also decided that anything encouraging 'excessive cruelty and morbidity' should also be banned. Some of the Grimms' fairy tales, including *The One who Wanted to Learn How to Shudder*, fell under this rubric. In fact, it had been used didactically to steel the Hitler Youth in classroom propaganda. One of the people who worked on the de-Nazification programme, Kathleen Davies, told me that the story should really be taken as a pub joke about a simpleton, the traditional *Dummling* of folk tales, the younger son who is so stupid he doesn't know that he should fear death. The ending with the bucket of water and the fishes is therefore a kind of broad joke. The minute you hear this sensible interpretation, you discover another context for the same story. Suddenly one can hear the voices ringing out with laughter: 'What ghosts and dead men couldn't do, a woman could! She knew how to put the fear of God into him.' The story also contains a germ of popular wisdom: 'He who does not know fear is a fool.' This, of course, offers a lesson in life that is the exact opposite of the Fascist attempt to train audiences in imperviousness to violence.

Though Bettelheim's book is full of riches and wisdom – and I for one owe to it a tremendous amount, as many of us do – there are problems with his analysis that fairy tales act therapeutically, assisting the child in adapting to maturity. *Celia*, for example, casts a strong, disturbing light on those problems, both in the ways in which it follows the Bettelheimian angle on fantasy, children and the uses of a terrifying fairy tale (in this case the Hobbyas), and the ways in which it diverges from it.

One of the problems in Bettelheim is that he presumes that the storyteller and the protagonist are united in their angle of vision, that they're in agreement, or that they're one and the same. We receive the story of *Cinderella* as hers, but in doing this we collapse the narrative voice into that of the heroine and consequently overlook that someone is telling Cinderella's story for her; or, indeed, given the circle of listeners around the storyteller or the audience in the cinema, telling it to her. The tale doesn't record the protagonist's own experience. Rather, a certain vision or viewpoint is projected through the tale to the audience, and a lesson is conveyed through the sympathy with the protagonist that the teller shows. In the case of *The One who Wanted to Learn How to Shudder*, as expounded by Nazi teachers, what we are talking about is their fantasies of evil and its embodiment in imagined enemies conjured by their own demons.

Celia, on the other hand, shows that the monsters aren't by any means always internal, psychotic fantasies. Beasts aren't only within, they can also be without. The fantasy of 'the other' isn't always a fantasy of the self as other, but rather can turn into an investigation of the other, a discovery and a confrontation. Celia identifies dangerous enemies to her world on two fronts – imaginary and real – threatening what she values and loves. But neither of them could be said to represent something beastly she fears or suspects inside herself. Nor, because we in the audience are on her side, do her feelings against these enemies appear groundless. When she identifies the punitive culling of rabbits with the Red-baiters who attack her neighbours the Tanners, and desires to save both her own rabbit, Murgatroyd, and her friend's next door, she finds the Hobbyas as the apt metaphor for their common enemy (whom she identifies with her Uncle John, the policeman, and her father who are collaborating both in the rabbit-culling and the Red-baiting). There is no possible interpretation, in terms of the character of Celia or of the film's logic, that can render Uncle John (or even her father) one of her internal demons with which she must come to terms.

In doing this, director Ann Turner contravenes psychoanalytic orthodoxy and makes a brilliantly gripping story out of Celia's personal use of enchantment. The murder, however, comes as a shock – not the assault on Uncle John itself, but its fatal effect – and after this the film does return to a kind of Bettelheimian obedience by showing the child heroine as a rather cool psychopath who restores harmony and order in the community of her peers by hanging a scapegoat as the murderer, in an almost Voodoo-like ritual. Storytelling, through the ritual enactment of hanging a scapegoat, becomes her way of dealing with the murder she has committed. The uses of enchantment, in this case, are wildly subversive in relation to orthodox morality and conduct. Fairy tale doesn't mould the little girl into acceptance, but offers her an instrument of revolt, of power, of delinquency. This make-believe, which does follow Bettelheim's idea of fantasy as therapy, remains thoroughly disturbing. Children's ability to smooth out the wrinkle of death is fine in the case of the innocent, but in the case of *Celia* it becomes troubling that it should be so effective.

I suspect that *Celia* as a film springs directly from its director's experiences in childhood, and that while nobody had actually been killed in the coincidence of events that the film records, Ann Turner had wanted murder most foul to sharpen the film's *frisson* – which it certainly does. But it also makes Celia, as a character, one of the affectless children of the contemporary cinema, thoughtlessly capable of recovering from cruelty and violence. It also calls sharply into question both the separateness of fantasy and reality, and the effects of fairy tale on fantasy. As Celia remains the object of our sympathies, she is portrayed in no way as alien, but rather as generic humanity embodied in childhood innocence. Her susceptibility to fairy tales' terrors, and her active response, provokes doubt in Bettelheim's thesis altogether. The uses of enchantment can indeed enable the child to defend herself, but not in the docile, adaptive manner he prescribed.

By this reversal *Celia* also exposes accurately the underlying premise in much of the psychoanalytic approach to fairy tale. Though Bettelheim takes the child's part, he wishes to use fairy tale to keep children in line, precisely because they are thought to be composed of monstrously-inclined raw material – polymorphously perverse psyches. The fairy tale is his method of confronting the beast in the child, handling it and taming it. This is why he can sometimes miss, with breathtaking lack of sympathy, the real sufferings of children in the stories. For Bettelheim, *Hansel and Gretel* is about learning to cope with the bad mother in one's mother, rather than it being about children abandoned to die in the forest, as unfortunately happened all too often among families suffering from poverty and starvation. Similarly, from this perspective, *Snow White* concerns Oedipal rivalry between mother and daughter, rather than chronicling stepmothers' historical antagonism against the children of an earlier marriage at a time when mothers often died in childbirth. And *Bluebeard* becomes a tale about rebellion against husbands, which young women must quell if they are to behave in a mature sexual way, rather than dealing with larger problems of sexual violence and cruelty within marriage.

But beasts are not always delusions or projections of the self as hateful. The fact that tyrannies conjure demons out of the innocent doesn't negate the fact that evils exist in the world out there and have to be dealt with. Fairy tale can offer a means to knowledge, rather than remaining a site where innocence is for ever preserved or, indeed, restored. Its fantasy turns a key to material survival, not only psychic maturity. And this is a dangerous power, so it matters very much who is the teller and why the tale is being told.

Celia does, of course, have a good internal beast: her totem animal, her pet rabbit which she hugs as part of herself in one of the key images from the film. In her other hand she holds the mask that empowers her magic, a mask that hung above the bed of her beloved grandmother who dies at the start of the film, the first of the Hobbyas's victims. The grandmother was, like the Tanners next door, a Communist, and after her death Celia's father savagely burns all her library of Marxist books – the first sacrilege against Celia's cherished internal symbols which he commits. It is important that the mask formed part of her grandmother's room and that Celia, like Red Riding Hood, aligns herself with the old woman against the monsters.

A continuity of female perspective is implied in terms of a tradition of storytelling. Women of different social status have collaborated on the invention and recounting of such material all over the world. The fame of people like the Grimm brothers and Charles Perrault has eclipsed the activity of many fellow women writers who took up fairy tale in both France and Germany in a spirit of defiance against the classicising academies, and constructed home-grown stories, sometimes in a language as close as possible to popular speech. The same can be said about British fairy tales; despite the fact that early collectors weren't especially interested in the sex of their sources, enough evidence exists to reveal that the telling of fairy tales in these islands was a woman's practice, too.

Italo Calvino was struck by the lively voices of illiterate women – laundresses, seamstresses – who contributed their tales to the collections he mined for his superb anthology *Fiabe Italiane* in 1956. Angela Carter has always been mindful of this aspect of the genre, and in *The Company of Wolves*, Neil Jordan's interpretation of her werewolf tales from *The Bloody Chamber*, the young girl's point of view mingles with the fairy godmother/grandmother character (Angela Lansbury) who acts as both curb and prompt to her imagination. Storytelling is an artisan's activity, as Walter Benjamin pointed out. It used to while away the tedium of home tasks – of spinning, weaving, cracking walnuts in the season. The poet Liz Lochhead remembers in one poem* a scene from her childhood:

No one could say the stories were useless
for as the tongue clacked
five or forty fingers stitched
corn was grated from the husk
patchwork was pieced
or the darning done . . .
the stories dissolved in the whorl of the ear
but they
hung themselves upside down
in the sleeping heads of the children
till they flew again
in the story-teller's night.

What does all this mean, and what relevance does it have to film?

---

* 'The Storyteller Poems', 1, from *Dreaming Frankenstein* (Edinburgh: Polygon Books, 1984), p. 70.

I would argue that film is essentially an oral medium and shares many characteristics with traditional storytelling. The camera acts as an anonymous narrator, in the same way as the teller of fairy tale does not comment on the action but holds to the matter-of-fact tone of the tale, concealing the shaping and directing of the material. At the same time, one of the sources of that shaping and directing lies in the circle of listeners, for the storyteller who does not please will not find an audience, or may even (as in the threat to Scheherazade) lose her head in the morning. In the same way, a film will cease to be shown if it fails to please, hence the practice of sneak previews, of sounding out audience response and then adjusting the plot to match (as, for instance, happened with *A Fish Called Wanda* when the series of squashed dogs offended sensibilities and was modified – ironic when you think of how many squashed women there are on film).

Robert Altman's unflinchingly cynical view of movie-making, *The Player*, dramatises exactly this opportunistic response of producers to audience needs, when the protagonist achieves full Hollywood success by delivering a happy ending. This may outrage those who believe in the integrity of the work and in individual imagination, but it conforms exactly to the practice of the village or bazaar storytellers who had to change an episode or ending if the circle around them melted away. Film has borne in mind the wishes of the audience in the same fashion. Méliès, in the notice he issued with the now lost version of *Red Riding Hood*, apologises for changing the end of the Perrault fairy tale, which he had otherwise followed with scrupulous respect. In Perrault, the wolf eats Red Riding Hood and that's that. 'Beware of Men', concludes the storyteller, 'especially when they smile and say sweet nothings.' But Méliès's heroine ends up safe and sound, because while the public can take a gobbled-up granny, the death of Little Red Riding Hood would have left 'une impression de malaise', an uneasy feeling. So in his film Méliès punishes the wolf instead.

Popular film offers a way into what was thought to be pleasing. It represents cloth cut to fit an audience's presumed preoccupations. This, too, is dangerous, and it becomes more dangerous the more monolithic the conditions of production. It is possible to discern in films that draw on fairy tale material the dance of male–female oppositions, the interlacing of the sexes' otherness vis-à-vis one another, and the co-option of fantasy into serving the possibility of harmony and happiness. In such films, the question: 'Who is telling the tale and to what purpose?' will often lead straight to an identification of the special interests of gender – to the voice of the grandmother, audible through the eyes of the child or adult protagonist, who holds up knowledge of adversaries and advantages to the younger generation and teaches them ways of dealing with them. These ways can be

24

resistant, Utopian, controversial, of course. But they can also fail to become imaginative or liberating, rather more expedient and safe, compliant with prevailing convention.

Although the audiences of spoken fairy tale were mixed, women seem to have predominated, as phrases like 'old wives' tales' reveal. And cinema, from its earliest days, attracted the enthusiasm of female spectators, rather to the surprise of early film impresarios who didn't expect footage of boxing matches to draw the crowds of women they did in the first decades of the century. However, this sense of 'knowing the other' goes far beyond the spectacle of boxing, and many early films use the medium's potential for fantasy rather than documentary to explore such possibilities. So when film departed from its role as chronicler of spectacular events and became a key to the inner world, women took part. The title for 'the first narrative film ever made' has been given to Alice Guy-Blaché for *La Fée au chou* (*The Cabbage Fairy*), made in 1896, but not as yet available for viewing. In Germany, Lotte Reiniger concentrated on fairy tales from East and West in her brilliantly crisp, inventive silhouette cartoons of the 20s.

II

The necessity of attracting an audience and pleasing the crowd influences the teller and shapes the story. In this respect, the development of fairy tale in film follows the developmental curve of the literary form, for early audiences were not only of both sexes but of mixed ages as well. Early films do not appear to target an age band (in the way that they do today, with ever more refined marketing techniques) any more than early printed collections of fairy tales from the 17th and 18th centuries singled out children as their readers.

Postulating a child as the protagonist as well as the receiver of the tale provided a metaphor for a certain ignorant, or innocent, state of mind, which by the end of the story will have been changed beyond recognition. These differences from contemporary fairy tale films and stories – the mixed age of the audience, the appeal to female as well as child sympathies, the consequently adult character of the material – maintained the genre's closer connection to harsh realities. The frame of the fairy tale made possible a certain outspokenness, the hope held out by the genre made possible frank confrontation of pain and torment. As Phaedrus said about fables as long ago as the first century AD: 'The slave, being liable to punishment for any offence, since he dared not say outright what he wished to say, projected his personal sentiments into fables and eluded censure under the guise of jesting with made-up stories.' The entertainment of movie fantasy, high jinks, special effects and magic can similarly disguise depths of outrage and anger.

The Wizard of Oz, made in 1925 by the popular comic Larry Semon, reveals the story's roots in the conditions of life in Kansas at the turn of the century much more keenly than the famous and much-loved Judy Garland version. Similarly, the early Renoir film La Fille de l'eau, an expressionist modern-dress recasting of the Cinderella story, is an ironical exercise in social comment of the kind we expect from its director. The escape to a fantasy land includes ordinary dreams – often a warm fire, a comfortable room, a clean bed, a full plate. There is no sense of sparing children's feelings or tenderness in this material. Fairy tales used to be for adults, who needed to lay bare the real in order to entertain the hope that change might be possible. Fantasy isn't only an escape, it can be a way in out of the cold.

As Angela Carter has written in the introduction to her witty and bracing collection The Virago Book of Fairy Tales, the goal of fairy tales is not a conservative but a Utopian one – a form of heroic optimism, as if to say 'One day we might be happy, even if it won't last.'

You will remember how in the 1939 Wizard of Oz, Dorothy declares at the end, 'There's no place like home,' and taps the heels of her ruby slippers in order to return to Kansas and to Aunt Em. But the 1925 version follows the Frank Baum book, first published in 1900, which is an undiluted family romance. A pretty much adult, seductively attractive Dorothy is the rightful Queen of Oz, who has been usurped by the wicked Wizard. Her Uncle Harry is pusillanimous and opportunist, quite ready to conspire with the Wizard to prevent her taking up the throne on her eighteenth birthday.

Frank Baum made some short Oz films before his death in 1909, and his son, who had the same name, collaborated with the then famous clown Larry Semon (who actually plays Baum in the framing story in which we see the creator making his characters as puppets) in the filming of this version which respects his father's beliefs more than the Victor Fleming favourite of 1939. For Frank Baum was a Utopian socialist and one of those mystic-minded feminists who yearned for matriarchy as the remedy of the world's ills. Oz represented the kingdom where feminine principles of justice and love would prevail once the usurpers were thrown out. Here Dorothy, played by the queenly Dorothy Duane (no white socks for her!) at the end of the film gains her just realm with Prince Kynd, her husband, once she has defeated the usurpers Lady Vishuss, Ambassador Wikked and Prime Minister Kruel. The villains mirror the powers that ruled Kansas, they embody the American urban crooks, bootleggers, mobsters, bosses and landlords who preyed on manual labourers like the workers on Uncle Harry's farm. The Scarecrow, the Tin Man and the Cowardly Lion in this film are only disguises for field-hands (including Oliver Hardy in a younger shape). Larry Semon combined movie tricks, vaudeville slapstick, terror and realism, in a way that would not have been considered suitable viewing for children by the time the later *Wizard* was made.

In the series of lectures he was actually giving when he died, Italo Calvino noted that a flight to another world is a common occurrence in oral folk tales. He developed this observation: 'Faced with the precarious existence of tribal life – drought, sickness, evil influences – the shaman responded by ridding his body of weight and flying to another world, another level of perception, where he could find the strength to change the face of reality.' For shaman read storyteller; to the circumstances that make life precarious, add the oppression of labour; and where women are concerned (and they are vitally con-cerned in the reception of movies) add sexual abuse and physical vulnerability. For Dorothy, the flight to Oz signifies escape from her uncle's attentions and, later, from the attempted forced marriage to Ambassador Wikked.

The events here are similar to those in Renoir's *La Fille de l'eau*, made in 1924. In this film, the heroine, meaningfully called Virginie, is assaulted by her Uncle Jeff. The inter-title announces: 'Uncle Jeff, a brute'. Virginie, like many fairy tale Cinderellas, is a motherless child. Her father accidentally drowns in the canal and she is left with Uncle Jeff who is drinking away all their money, and so eventually has to put up for sale the barge on which they live to meet his debts. She approaches him in his bunk, in order to ask what they are going to do, and he gets a lascivious look in his eye and assaults her. The constricted space of the cabin makes their fight all the more ferocious, as she puts up a spirited resistance to his attempts. The scene is unbear-ably prolonged; she only just manages to run away. But it avoids the gloating on violence and hypocritical posturings of outrage which mark some contemporary films. The sequence ends with the uncle and a crony exchanging drunken resolutions to deal out punishment to the girl. Renoir doesn't scant the nastiness of his villains or present their aggressiveness in a heroic light.

You may think that I'm stretching fairy tale as a genre to fit anything I like, finding Cinderellas and Bluebeards here, there and everywhere. And Renoir's heightened dramatic style exudes an atmosphere of viol-ent realism which we aren't accustomed to associate with the fairy tale. But the never-never land, bright as sweet wrappers and crowned with towers or castles, long ago and far away, does not only define the territory of fairy tale. The circumstances of telling, and the function of holding out hope, are two much more suggestive and reliable ways

27

to distinguish the genre. Renoir's fairy tale was rooted in the humdrum and even squalid material circumstances of life, and this early film helps the viewer today to understand how such romances as *La fille de l'eau* used the formulaic rags-to-riches tale to represent contemporary conditions – of child-abusers and drunkards, of Gypsies and their enemies, of maidservants and the hazards of their life. Renoir knew he was telling a fairy story. He was interested in such tales as conventional frames in which he could say what he wanted to say (often about *la bêtise humaine*, human folly) and also experiment with the medium's potential for erotic and consolatory fantasy.

In Calvino's novel *Invisible Cities*, the emperor is listening to Marco Polo's traveller's tales about imaginary places far and wide. Suddenly the emperor reproaches him: 'Your cities do not exist. Perhaps they have never existed. Why do you amuse yourself with consolatory fables? I know well that my empire is rotting like a corpse in a swamp, whose contagion infects the crows that peck it as well as the bamboo which grows. . . . Why do you not speak to me of this?' To this Marco Polo responds: 'Yes, the empire is sick. And what is worse, it is trying to become accustomed to its sores. This is the aim of my explorations, *examining the traces of happiness still to be glimpsed.*'

Bearing this in mind, let's return to *La Fille de l'eau*. After Virginie has run away from her brutal uncle, she meets up with a Gypsy poacher and his pipe-smoking mother who befriend her and teach her how to survive. Later, the Gypsies are themselves attacked and their caravan is burned down. They then abandon Virginie to her own devices (again Renoir refuses sentimentalisation) and she finds herself once again alone and vulnerable. She wanders through the night and finally falls back exhausted against a tree and begins to dream. In her delirium both the poacher and her uncle appear to torment and terrorise her, in a surrealist montage of looming faces and distorted and grimacing close-ups. Renoir visualises the dream in a disconnected series of spaces: first the forest, then a nightmare colonnade, and Virginie constantly seeking to escape. A 'prince' appears to rescue her, the son of a bourgeois family in the neighbourhood who is actually looking for her in the forest, and carries her off on a white charger, which again the camera follows against an abstracted, almost empty background as if they were flying through the air.

However, even in this benign section of the erotic dream sequence – Virginie with the prince and the white charger – what is interesting is that she seems so cramped and in pain. Renoir has qualified her fantasy of escape and shown her still to be in torment, in her delirium in the forest.

La Fille de l'eau does have a happy ending, and I think it actually offers a subtext to Jean Vigo's *L'Atalante*, which was made nine years later and which also begins on a barge and ends in bliss. But while Renoir, who was Vigo's mentor, portrays the bargee and the poacher as brutal, in contrast to the polite bourgeois world into which Virginie escapes as civilised, Vigo is actually affirming that the labouring class is capable of profound feelings too.

The Beast makes itself manifest as both social and sexual oppressor in *The Wizard of Oz* and *La Fille de l'eau*, made at different ends of the movie world but around the same time. The impulse behind telling such stories is a desire for change. Larry Semon was so doubtful that Dorothy and Prince Kynd would succeed in regaining their rightful kingdom that in the very last shot of the film he shows them chased again out of Oz, tumbling through the sky – the cycle beginning again. Similarly, Renoir, in the next fairy tale he made, chose Hans Christian Andersen's tragedy *The Little Matchgirl*, and filmed the child freezing to death in the snow as she dreams of food and firelight and toys made in the form of perfect golden-haired little girls with party frocks and shoes.

III

The Wizard of Oz and *La Fille de l'eau*, like many fairy tales, tell the story of an all-important move in women's lives: the departure from the natal or paternal house and its exchange with another man's house. The stories begin with the heroine in one place and end with her in another, and in this respect are women's stories, founded in the social principle of female exogamy or marrying-out for women. The Beast's castle in such tales (both on film and in print) commands as much attention and awe as the beast himself, whether it is Bluebeard's castle or Jean's barge in *L'Atalante*. In fact, in many ways *L'Atalante* most closely resembles the Beauty-and-Beast cycle of fairy tales. The coffin-shaped barge Juliette enters is a confined bridal chamber, one in a long tradition of marital cells which fairy tale brides enter in stories like *Bluebeard* or *Beauty and the Beast*, and where they have to come to terms with their husband – or flee him.

The beginning of *L'Atalante* shows the wedding guests like so many mourners at a pinched and ghastly funeral. The scene has a kind of absurdist black humour about it, but nevertheless remains joyless, an alarming scene of severance with Jean as a kind of Pluto and Juliette as his Proserpine carried off into the darkness of his underwater kingdom. We later see Juliette, the reluctant bride, on the barge for the first time, and then with Jean, before their love develops, scared in her groom's funereal vessel. This cramped underworld is full of chambers and surprising inhabitants: dozens of cats (a recurrent symbol of

29

the night), and of wonders and horrors which awaken the new bride to knowledge. In a remarkable improvised sequence, Père Jules, played by Michel Simon, takes her on a tour of his cabinet of curiosities, including the tattoos on his belly. The Beauty's discovery of the Beast's treasures in her new home usually precedes her growing knowledge of him and feeds her fears.

The terrors and excitements of the bride's state are metonymically contained in the groom's house, his castle. The transferral from one to the other constitutes the central experience of the fairy tale heroine, as it in turn constituted the most crucial event in women's lives until the present century made a greater degree of independence possible. Sexual initiation combined with a change of social identity, a new family and a new domicile. One reason why Judy Garland's Dorothy must return to Kansas and her own backyard is that, unlike her predecessor, she is not old enough to marry or to strike out on her own and find happiness elsewhere (in the atmosphere of the times when the film was made).

The heroine's actual transition often corresponds to the flight to another world which the shaman accomplishes. The gateway to fantasy (and especially erotic fantasy) when translated to screen is opened in sleep or dreams. The dreaming woman becomes a key figure in fairy tale movies. It is through fantasy, through the uses of enchantment, that she achieves her passage from one state to another, that she manages to tame or otherwise come to terms with the Beast. The cinema's capacity to represent this state in material imagery can serve to communicate her transition. We are shown her terror from her point of view by entering a dream state – as in the case of Virginie in *La Fille de l'eau*, or in that of *Die Marquise von O*, Rohmer's erotic version of *The Sleeping Beauty*, or again in the case of Belle from Cocteau's classic *La Belle et la bête*. The dreaming heroine, often considered a mere passive victim, shouldn't be underestimated. There is a sense that she is voyaging, and that the film we are watching (or the story we are hearing) emerge from her fantasy. In the same way as the child now dominates as the wise eye of unspoilt witness on the screen, the woman used to. In both these motifs, of course, the influence of surrealism can be felt.

Significantly, male directors have responded vividly to the fraught nature of this transition. Their interest may spring from the necessary role it grants many men's lives as fathers and bridegrooms, and from the subtle accusation as well that beastliness lies in the eye of the beholder, that dreaming brides conjure their own demons and that men are not responsible. When the brides wake, they will realise the truth. Here, the psychoanalytical interpretation favoured in most fairy tale films can devolve responsibility from the male on to the female, representing the bride as deluded in her fantasy, not wise.

Several films have also explored, perhaps understandably, the danger of the heroine's predicament when she has no castle to keep her, when the Beast she encounters prevents her movement out of the parental home, or when she cannot exchange father for groom – because one or the other has transgressed against their appointed role. For example, Jacques Démy's lighthearted, witty, decorative homage to Cocteau's *La Belle et la bête*, the 1971 film *Peau d'âne (Donkey Skin)*, explores the original Perrault fairy tale of the title, which is based on a very ancient folk tale about a king who wants to marry his daughter. Here, the father (played by Jean Marais, who was the Beast in Cocteau's film so there's an intertextual reference here) usurps the role of the Beast. This king's power derives from his magic donkey which shits gold. The princess, played by Cathérine Deneuve, asks for the hide of this precious beast as a condition of the proposed incestuous marriage, and unexpectedly her father agrees to destroy the source of his own wealth and give it to her. She subsequently flees from his castle wearing the symbol of her father's crime and authority and fortune, and passes a certain period in the wilderness as a swineherd, reviled for her filth and sluttishness by all, until she finds her prince and takes possession of his castle.

Before his death in 1990, Jacques Démy participated in the making of *Jacquot de Nantes*, a film about his childhood, directed by his wife Agnès Varda. It recalls how he was taken to see fairy tale puppet shows as a child and how he himself played with toy theatres with the help of his grandmother, even staging his own *Cinderella*. A film like *Peau d'âne*, for all its trappings of the fairy tale *fantastique* and its once-upon-a-time distancing manner, enfolds within it a kind of critique of the Oedipal fantasy theory. In its pretty, flirtatious way, it plumbs very powerful material. Démy uses enchantment with high spirits, a sense of fun and a light heart. But it doesn't prevent him (rather, it helps him) dramatise the daughter's rejection of her father, rather than her fantasy of love for the father which is how the fairy tale *Donkey Skin* is usually interpreted in psychoanalytical material – that is to say, it is presented as a transferred fantasy, and a desiring daughter imagines that her father is in love with her.

One of the few recent films to retain the fierce intensity of folklore's relationship to the circumstances of life (rather than ascribe terrors to female fantasy alone) is Eric Rohmer's *Die Marquise von O*. It restores rape to the heart of the fairy tale. Again in this film, the act of the Beast protagonist prevents the orderly transition of the heroine out of her father's house, to assume a new social identity in a regular fashion. In the medieval legends which inspired Perrault's famous *Sleeping Beauty* tale, the prince makes love to the beautiful princess while she still lies in her enchanted sleep. It is one of the twins she bears as a result, trying to suck at her breast but finding her finger instead, that draws the splinter that spellbound her and so wakes her up. In the seventeenth-century Neopolitan version, the prince is already married; he simply kills his first wife, because she's failed to bear him any children, when he finds that he has this new, delightful family with whom he'd like to spend some time. This is the kind of vigorous cynicism that proved thoroughly enjoyable to the crowds in 1636, but is so shocking to us today that I can confidently predict it will never be retold in a version of *Sleeping Beauty* made by Disney or any other company in children's entertainment.

In Rohmer's film, which follows the short story by the German Romantic writer, Kleist, the tale turns on honour. Its subtle exploration of aristocratic morality and immorality make the heroine a courageous innocent who is able to confront society after she's been drugged and then assaulted by her supposed deliverer. The erotic dimension, lost in the retellings of *Sleeping Beauty* at a later date, returns sharply in this intense film about the differences between male and female desire. In one sense, the Marquise von O learns to love the Beast, in spite of everything (and he to love her), as in *L'Atalante*. Wronged heroines can come to different ends, and this happy ending is one of the most popular and common conclusions to fairy tale romances.

Cinderella's close cousin in folklore – Beauty, of the *Beauty and the Beast* cycle of stories – learns love with her Beast and transforms him, rather than doing away with him by some or other means such as murder in *Celia* or flight in *La Fille de l'eau*. In some ways, the films which deal with this tale show her cured of fantasy and her terrors banished as empty. The traditional Beast's character in such films has generally been edited and moulded in the same way as in versions written for children from the 19th century onwards (and women have contributed to this belief in romance as a healing process). The softening of attitudes towards the monster groom gradually increases in the literary history of the tale, and the accompanying lesson that wives should learn – to love their spouses – becomes louder and louder. In this, too, the development of the fairy tale film follows the written tradition, as films in which the Beast turns out not to be a beast at all become more frequent and more popular. The pattern follows the gradual establishment of marriage by inclination over the arrangements and forced marriages of the Middle Ages and the Renaissance. But it also reflects a new singling out of a young audience and the establishment of fairy tales' pedagogical function.

The most familiar version of *Beauty and the Beast* was written in the mid-18th century by Mme Leprince de Beaumont, who had left an unhappy marriage in France to come to England on her own and work as a governess here to aristocratic English girls. In 1756 she first produced a volume of stories for the education of young women. It was called *The Misses' Magazine* (so you see that she's already targeting young women). She wrote, for example, watered down reinterpretations of Richardson's *Clarissa*. Cocteau's *La Belle et la bête* followed quite faithfully Mme de Beaumont's tale. She was, above all, concerned with the moral development of young women faced with marriages over which they had almost no control, and the story can be read as an attempt to persuade them that they could make the best of this alarming prospect, that love could grow from disadvantageous beginnings, that inside the Beast who might be given to them as a husband there might be true love. This didactic, wishful strain grows apace in the 19th century. It reaches its apogee in the analysis of Bettelheim, who believes that Beauty should have been grateful to her father for relinquishing his 'Oedipal attachment' and handing her over to the Beast.

From the end of the 17th century onwards, children are increasingly identified as the appropriate audience for fairy tales, a movement which can also be discerned in later fairy tale films. Perhaps the surprising thing about this is that women contribute strongly to the literature of adaptation, tolerance and compassion for the Beast, and this is reflected in the films which adapt their stories, like Cocteau's classic. We may not particularly want to hear this, as we search for heroines of spirit, but many of the popular retellings of *Beauty and the Beast* which followed Mme de Beaumont were also by high-minded ladies intent (in Angela Carter's fine phrase) on 'housetraining the Id'. Mary Lamb translated the tale into English around 1811. She was Charles Lamb's sister and in a fit of insanity had actually murdered her own mother. Adelaide Doyle, sister of Dickie Doyle the fairy painter, produced another version a few decades later. Lucy Crane helped her brother Walter with his fairy tales, including a famous full-colour version of *Beauty and the Beast*. Andrew Lang's version, printed in the first of the highly successful series of fairy tale books (the series which every nineteenth-century middle-class household had), was composed for him by Miss Minnie Wright. Such stories are filled with intergenerational female warnings about the nature of love and the need for conformity. It is important to restore this level of meaning to them when watching the film versions.

Jean Marais's Beast in Cocteau's film embodies the pitifulness of the common condition which art and love and beauty can redeem by transformation. The wishfulness of the romance doesn't entirely obscure the matrimonial transactions of which Mme de Beaumont was acutely aware. Beauty offers herself in order to save her father's life and fortune. Nevertheless, the film's aestheticised artifice perfectly represents the long-held ideal that civilisation can be achieved through courtly romance, an ideal to which women have contributed since the courts of love were held in Blanche of Castille's day.

In one type of story, like *La Belle et la bête*, the disenchantment of the Beast (his regaining human and consequently lovable shape) depends on the attitude of Beauty, on her heart and her goodness. *She* has to change in order to change him. The making of the Beast into a man entails the making of Beauty into a wife. This commitment to an ideal femininity as the condition of romance in civilisation is an enormous subject. But as a theme it was, of course, a gift to the audience who identified with the Beast, and films have since developed, in any number of ingenious ways, the point of view of the Beast rather than that of the bride, and have told the story of a woman wooed by an unlikely suitor who in the end either wins her or loses her in tragic circumstances. He is often winning and cuddly – the Beast as soft toy, as teddy bear, as misunderstood waif. This theme was taken up by the writer–producer Caroline Thompson with *Edward Scissorhands* – like Frankenstein's creature, he's an artefact born of man not woman, and he also suffers from having dangerous cutlery for hands. Misunderstood by the suburban households where he finds himself, he is driven back into his castle. Again, as in Mary Shelley's founding fantasy of Frankenstein, masculine strength far outstrips its own desires. Edward is really only interested in beautifying women with new haircuts, not raping them with his tremendous threatening tools.

These women writers and film-makers are attracted to redemptive fantasy *per se*, the refashioning of menace by imaginative acts of identification with the male. Whether it is collusion with the structures of oppression, or strategies of resistance, it is a phenomenon which naturally appeals to the men in the audience as well, since it paints them, however apparently beastly, as tender and loving and misunderstood.*

Fairy tale has offered a way of saying the unsayable, speaking the unspeakable: the incestuous love of a father for his daughter; the assault of a woman by an officer who pretended to be her rescuer; the abandonment of children by their parents. It shares these possibilities with the audience, mingles its knowledge with theirs, issues warnings and makes promises. The uses of enchantment are complex, but the aim of social adaptation, which Bettelheim stressed as their principal salutary function, narrows the possibilities too much and underestimates their power. As a popular medium, fairy tale film can offer

---

* See my article, 'Beauty and the Beast', *Sight and Sound*, October 1992, for a review of the Disney film version and reflections on this theme.

channels of resistance to the Beast in many guises, as well as other magical ways of dealing with him.

To conclude, I want to mention a sequence from a British trick film of 1914, called *The Magic Glass*, which offers a metaphor for the act of looking, for the cinematic spectacle. A child, whose point of view we share, discovers that his father has invented a magic glass which enables the user to see through doors. His father is a skinflint who denies his mother what she needs. He also punishes the boy without good reason, to the mother's misery. But there's no doubt whose side we in the audience are meant to be on. The magic glass acts like the movie camera itself, the ultimate voyeur's instrument. The child switches the glass with his mother's lorgnette. When we see what the boy and his mother see, as his predecessor the butler did, we are no longer peeping with male eyes through a hood into the diorama of a seaside pier, but looking invisibly, with the fantasy power of the cinema. And what do we see through the mother's glass? The father sexually harassing the maid! I think it's fair to infer that the exposure of the father pleased the maids and the wives in the audience. The joke is on him. However, the boy is subsequently punished for his peeping, serving perhaps to soothe the feathers of the men in the audience who may have felt ruffled by the female chortles and the slur on their authority.

Like the magic glass in this short, cinema can't be held exclusively by the heads of households: it can fall into the hands of the ground-lings and give them a certain new-found power of fantasy, retaliation and knowledge. The boy in *The Magic Glass* is the innocent eye who learns something and is able to set matters to right and turn the tables on the culprit (for a brief moment) through his mother's glass and the uses of enchantment. The fantasy here lies in seeing itself, not in what is seen.

35

THROUGH A CHILD'S EYES

Internal BFI Seminar, 12 February 1992

Marina Warner

This lecture follows on from 'The Uses of Enchantment'. It will be arranged in two parts, each focusing on a particular issue. First, 'Childhood as Point of View'; secondly, and I hope this will not seem too oblique, a consideration of the early tale of *Cupid and Psyche*, a romance written in Latin in the second century.

I

Though the films I've chosen for the NFT season are interpretations of fairy tales, I'm not specifically going to talk about fairy tale today, and I'm not going to pick films which target children as their audience – though some films which I am going to talk about include children in their audience. The ones I'll concentrate on are films in which a child, or children, feature, often at the centre of the narrative, while at the same time (and even more crucially) acting as the narrator. That is to say, films in which we see the action through the perspective of the child.

The paradigm for this kind of point of view (certainly one of the more eloquent and extraordinary examples of it in fiction) can be found in Henry James's *What Maisie Knew*. On page one of the first chapter James writes:

> She [Maisie] was taken into the confidence of passions on which she fixed just the stare she might have for images bounding across the wall in the slide of a magic lantern. Her little world was phantasmagoric, strange shadows dancing on a sheet. It was as if the whole performance had been given for her, a mite of a half-scared infant in a great dim theatre.

The book has a complicated history in terms of its writing. James began work on it in the 1890s but it wasn't finally published in its definitive version until 1907. So, interestingly enough, its genesis corresponds with the beginning of cinema as an entertainment. Maisie, for those who haven't read the novel, is an early heroine in a story of a custody battle; she's a child in a tug of war between her parents, to whose actions she bears witness. At the beginning of the book she's five years old, but the time span of the narrative is rather difficult to determine so we don't actually know how old she is at the end. However, during the course of these years she witnesses her parents' marriages, remarriages, affairs, and the different shapes and configurations of their struggle over her. She always remains someone who doesn't fully understand, and it is through her that we see the action, forcing us into a continual position of irony – that we as adult readers understand more than Maisie knew. It also remains a conundrum exactly what Maisie does know.

She sees the dance of her rather corrupt and squalid parents' love affairs as phantoms dancing on a screen, James tells us, as if in a magic lantern. But these phantoms are in a sense themselves doubled: they're both the actual actions of her divorcing and struggling parents, but they're also in some way implied to be her fantasy. We're never quite sure if what she sees is what's actually happening, or if we're seeing only what she imagines to be happening. That is absolutely essential to the ambiguities and ironies of the book.

This notion – that it could all be her fantasy – returns us to the idea that we are seeing everything through her eyes. So it's not the world, but rather the child who is the screen on which the phantoms are projected. In that sense a doubling occurs here, too: in seeing through the eyes of the child we become both camera and screen at the same time. And as these sights unfold, so the child's experience grows and we're let into the process of growing up, of learning, of character-formation, of subjectivity. There is a way in which the child's experience tells the story. She goes from, as it were, degree zero to some degree of knowledge. The last sentence of *What Maisie Knew* reopens the question with which the whole book has dealt: what exactly does Maisie know? The final question mark is crucial. And that is very much the form in which some of the films I am going to talk about are themselves constructed, when they use the child to take us on a journey of discovery.

A successful, powerful and absolutely emblematic, indeed literal, use of this strategy in the cinema occurs in Peter Weir's film *Witness*, in which the murder in the men's lavatory at the beginning is seen only by the child and by us, the audience. The film also functions at an allegorical level: the idea of the child witness intensifies the audience's view that the Amish are also seen as innocent, like young children themselves; because their pre-industrial, collective way of life echoes some Ur state of harmony, of idyllic relations. The Amish are the youth of America who somehow have been preserved in their perfect innocence. And Kelly McGillis, who plays the mother of the boy who witnesses the crime, embodies innocent womanhood, too. She exists in some paradise untainted by present-day American corruption, which corresponds to the child's consciousness before adult actions corrupt that innocent eye.

Another rather different type of film, but also similar in its use of the child as witness, is Michael Verhoeven's *The Nasty Girl*, in which we see the unfolding of a corrupt adult world, this time through the eyes of a schoolgirl who wanders into it unwittingly. We again experience a double consciousness of what is happening because, while we expect there to have been Fascist activity in the village, she stumbles across it rather innocently. But she's actually much less innocent than Maisie. I shall return to *The Nasty Girl* later on when I discuss the issue of childhood curiosity as a leverage against archetypal fixity. It's rather different from *Witness* in that respect, but it retains the same kind of storytelling construction.

This use of the child as our eyes depends on two strong themes in the history of the representation of childhood, or in the understanding of what childhood is. Firstly, the idea that the child is innocent: a *tabula rasa*, a blank screen (again the self-reflective image of the cinema) on which experience makes its, usually dirty, mark. There are numerous linguistic uses which reinforce this. For example, the old Christian idea of the soul, which is so often expressed in the diminutive, so that the soul which is first issued from the hand of the Creator in Dante, for instance, is called the *animula*, the 'little soul', and *blanda*, 'white'. This idea of candour, innocence, whiteness, littleness, belongs to a moral ideal that is typified by the child.

One of the things that happens in the idea of the journey of the soul (which I shall subsequently develop, and which is mirrored in these kinds of stories such as *Witness*, *What Maisie Knew* and so forth) is that the *tabula rasa* is changed and shaped and moved by certain events. It's written on, scrawled on, defaced, and, in the process, arrives at individuation. But at a cost. The outcome is a kind of differentiation, allowing individuality to emerge. Very often the signs of this arrival of specific individuality are very closely linked to carnal knowledge, which is why so many of these films are often about sexual initiation. And that sexual knowledge usually comes with the arrival of self-consciousness of gender. This self-consciousness also then circumscribes what actions this character is permitted.

So that's one idea: the idea of innocence, that childhood innocence then falls or rises into a form of consciousness which is in a way determined by sexual labelling.

The second thing which this idea of the child as witness (and the person through whom we see) depends on, is a very long-established notion of the child's closer intimacy with the irrational and with fantasy. These two aspects of childhood are in a sense in conflict, and the conflict can be identified in documents going right back to the Middle Ages, and no doubt earlier than that. St Paul, for example, says 'When I was a child I spoke as a child, and now that I'm a man I've put away childish things' – the idea that you must cease to be a child if you are to be a proper, full person in Christ. The whole doctrine of original sin means that you must set aside the original taint, the original childishness which marks you and prevents you from being a fully operating Christian spirit. In 1555 a Christian scholar called Luis de Granada wrote: 'What is a child save a lower animal in the form of man?' In consequence of this inherent baseness and sinfulness of the child, we have a horrendous history of childhood discipline, usually believed, in good faith, to be what was necessary to make children human. The Puritans are a classic example. If you read the diary of someone like Cotton Mather, he beat his beloved daughter continually – then wrote about it in grief. But he considered that he was saving her soul and must do it for her good. It's because children are given to wantonness and indiscipline and lack of restraint that they have no natural Christian life in them unless they are beaten. This is all to do with the fantasy that the child partakes of the diabolical, which must be curbed and disciplined and corralled into proper social behaviour.

But God's little enemies at heart had, at the same time, a number of very significant champions, not the least of whom was Jesus. There are several texts in the Gospels, much cited by people who felt more compassionate towards children, in which Jesus holds up children as the ideal pattern of human nature. Among the most famous are 'Suffer the little children to come unto me,' and 'Except ye be contented, and become as little children, ye shall not enter the kingdom of heaven.'

This recovery of belief in a child's intrinsic goodness became particularly popular in the 17th century, which is interesting because it actually coincides or converges with the development of fairy tale literature in print for children and the first publications aimed at entertaining and edifying them as a special audience. Furthermore, quite a lot of the fairy tale literature for children emerging at the end of the 17th century and thereafter borrows for the frontispiece the story-telling scene, the iconography of Christ as the Sermon on the Mount. There is a sense in which the storyteller, as represented in those familiar images of children surrounding the narrator in the frontispieces of the earliest books of fairy tales, comes to look a little bit like Jesus surrounded by the little children.

In 1628, for instance, the Bishop of Salisbury, John Earle, wrote lovingly of children:

His father hath writ him his own little story, wherein he reads those days of his life that he cannot remember, and sighs to see what innocence he has outlived. The older he grows, he is a stair lower from God. The child is a man in a small letter, yet the best copy of Adam before the fall.

This idea that the child represents some prelapsarian ideal, some image of humanity before it fell into sin, actually informs the later elevation of the child, too. The commitment of the Romantics to imagination, to fantasy as the instrument of truth, led them to this idea of the child who could provide an unspoiled, undoctored, spontaneous response to the world. This you can find in a number of texts. It's very strong in Victor Hugo, for example: *Les Misérables* is a prime text of innocence, goodness and the energy of children. Other examples include Coleridge's poems to his son, or Christina Rossetti's *Goblin Market*, and the many poems about how children have an access to the other world – they can go through the constraining walls by means of a mixture of their presocial moral sense and their untutored individual fantasy.

And, of course, at the beginning of the 19th century, you have the Grimm brothers in Germany generally angling their work towards children. The Grimms created a different strand of fairy tale transmission by thinking of the stories not as a literature of mixed audiences but as literature with a particular pedagogical function. Their attitude towards the child, as a vehicle both for the supernatural and of moral behaviour, is reflected very strongly today in the work of Maurice Sendak, one of the most popular of children's writers and illustrators. In addition to illustrating the Grimms' tales, Sendak has also written numerous scary stories with strange, almost prophetic, children as their heroes and heroines. In one of his books, *Outside Over There*, which was about a changeling child, his iconographic style imitates Philip Otto Runge who was one of the German Romantics and used child symbolism himself in a number of visionary allegorical paintings like *New Day*, in which the child symbolises the new age, the age before the time of the Fall. Film has absorbed, it seems to me, this Romantic child as symbol, so in a sense there is that mixed and ambiguous position of the supernatural and the moral in both aspects, as immoral and premoral and radiantly sinless at one and the same time, as an image of hope and despair.

In 'The Cry of the Children' (1843), a rather typical, sentimental sort of Victorian poem, Elizabeth Barrett Browning wrote:

But the young, young children, O my brothers,
They are weeping bitterly!
They are weeping in the playtime of the others,
In the country of the free.

Now she was probably referring here to contemporary child labour. But at the same time she was also allegorising the human condition in a particular way that I think we have directly inherited: this idea that the child knows something better than we do, while at the same time possessing an innocence that is constantly being assailed and consequently suffering. The child both mirrors our potential and represents what we have forfeited. Therefore the child's mind, if one can enter it, holds the key to something beyond the reality principle. This passing beyond the reality principle through the eyes of the child offers hope and change, which is one of the principal functions of the fairy tale. Novalis, who was one of the first Germans to become very interested in the genre, wrote: 'Our life is no dream, but it should and will perhaps become one.'

The self-deluding aspects of such romancing have been criticised, from both political and feminist points of view, throughout the century. Dreaming prevents action, reconciles people to their lot, stuffs them full of hopeless, fatalistic yearning. Raymond Williams, for instance, writing about pastoral nostalgia in *The Country and the City*, comments that every generation looks back to a better time when there was greater justice, more harmony, in a land when nature was greener, and this vision of the past was a perpetual sort of perennial myth in English poetry. He has a surprising comment to make on this kind of nostalgia:

There have been powerful spokesmen in every period for the intermediate classes. These varying – sometimes unconscious – identifications matter, for it is in their light that we must examine both the reactions to disturbance and the recurrent myth of a happier and more natural past.

'These varying – sometimes unconscious – identifications' catches one of the Utopian aspects of fantasy. For Williams is attempting here to analyse why so many poets, who are not actually implicated themselves in the life of the labouring classes, saw the life of Gypsies or of people working on the land as a way of reclaiming some earlier state of bliss which their lives somehow touched. And Williams actually defends this. He does not interpret it as a kind of cultural annexation by a higher literate class or a lower illiterate class, but rather sees that the attempt to sympathise with them offers an important avenue of social transformation. I think that this model can be applied to the presence of children as a mediating consciousness in film. By seeing the world through the eyes of children we are attempting to slough off our own fallen nature and return to some dream possibility: 'to remake the world in the image of desire', as Gillian Beer has written about Romance as a literary form.

Therefore, the more tragic and disturbing a story is, the greater the sadness, the greater the fall from the possible happiness at the end. So, for example, *Witness* leaves us with a tragic sense of our own condition, in spite of the romantic ending. When a child is vitiated, is tarnished in a film, the irony of loss has already been built in because the child should be untouched or innocent. The whole presence of the child is founded on the axiomatic idea that children should symbolise innocence. There you have the added *frisson*. In a film like *The Omen* or *Rosemary's Baby* the twist is already built in, because evil is present in what should be the pattern of innocence.

In a way, I think it's probably easier to sustain an empirical argument about the innocence of children than it is to observe the perceived, intrinsic connection of children with fantasy. The idea that children have this close link with the fantastic seems to me to offer a metaphorical way of thinking about adult irrationalism and dreams – of denying that these are adult, that irrationality is an adult condition – and to distance them as childish is a form of oppression itself. In my life, certainly, irrationalism and dreams have never ceased to both torment me and give me pleasure.

But the correlation (very much supported by psychoanalysis) has ensured that the category of the fantastic seems to belong to children. Therefore when adults want to represent it they mask themselves as children. The child who appears, who acts, who is seen in the film, is therefore caught between adult sentimentality about childhood and the violence of sexuality, of fantasies which are permitted culturally to the child but denied a mature person. One of the consequences of this has been that the continuing association of children with fairy tale, and the kinds of savage fantasies contained in fairy tales, has deepened the identification of the category 'child' with cruelty, grisliness and pleasure in horror, which again is a sort of false consciousness about children, as distinct from adults.

I hope I've demonstrated that I think that behind the child narrator very definitely lurks the adult, man or woman. Very often in these films in which we follow the child's point of view, the story told is actually the film-maker's story. They are transparently autobiographical, or they are open biography claiming to be such, and they are in that sense stories of the making of the self. There is a direct use of the first person in the child's voice, which is sometimes actually based on a book. In that case, one adult may be impersonating another, or they can be, as I have said, the direct personal recollection written and directed by the very same person. There are quite a number of these films: Vigo's *Zéro de Conduite*, Cocteau's *Les Enfants terribles*, *My Life as a Dog*, written and directed by Lasse Halstrom, *Celia*, which may or may not be autobiographical but certainly coincides in date with Ann Turner's childhood in Melbourne during the fifties. I don't know if Emir Kusturica's *When Father Was Away on Business* is autobiographical or not, but it contains one of the most wonderful scenes, technically reproducing the child's point of view – he listens to the adults' conversations from a position under the table, with the camera taking his viewpoint. Of course, a very important technical aspect of these films is that they often adopt a low camera angle.

An Angel at my Table, based on Janet Frame's trilogy of her life and directed by Jane Campion, offers a very interesting example of a doubling of the autobiography, a film in which the film-maker filters a personal memoir through another person's life story – I can think of other examples, like Louis Malle's *Au Revoir les enfants*. But *An Angel at my Table* contains a very striking scene, in which the teacher recites Tennyson's 'Morte d'Arthur'. It is a spellbinding episode, and one which conveyed to me very powerfully the gender of the director, because the actress who played the teacher was heavily made-up with raven hair and quite a prominent nose, and was exactly the physical type of female (an older woman, with dyed hair, extravagantly painted) who usually personifies something malignant. Yet this scene was done with incredible goose-bump passion, it was absolutely thrilling, and you felt the total commitment of the class, how they got swept up in the dream of the Lady in the Lake as the sword came out of the water. And afterwards, by sheer chance, a friend of mine who is a New Zealander told me that the actress playing the teacher was Jane Campion's own mother who had been a very famous actress in New Zealand but had tragically suffered a series of severe nervous breakdowns and had stopped acting. So in *An Angel at my Table*, Jane Campion has, in a very interesting way, doubled her own experience of mental breakdown by making a film about Janet Frame's mental breakdown, in which her mother has a role which restores to her what she had lost from her own breakdown. And I for one find that extremely powerful.

The dramatic ironies of the child's point of view are manifold. First of all, the child's ignorance of what is happening puts the audience constantly in a guilty position of knowing something that the child

Celia (Ann Turner, 1988)

or children are not in a position to grasp, which of course intensifies the poignancy – or, if the film is a comedy, intensifies the humour. Secondly, the child's superior wisdom, the assumed vantage point of innocence and the greater access to fantasy, leaves the adults in the audience to see their own absurdity and harshness through the eyes of the child. So there develops a self-critical irony, which is very strong in *Zéro de Conduite*, for example. Thirdly, there is the child's anarchic state of exclusion from convention. It's noticeable that child heroes or heroines are very rarely goody-goodies: they're almost always marginalised, delinquent, off centre or misunderstood in some way. The contrast between the two little girls in *Celia* – between Celia as the one who doesn't pray when all the others do, who doesn't toe the line, and her cousin whose father she kills – provides a highly typical contrast between the dutiful child and the disobedient child.

This sort of anarchic consciousness posits the child as a sort of romantic *étranger*, a stranger through whom we in the audience are permitted to touch the magic of being strangers as well, and this 'strangerdom' becomes, through the child, a reservoir of strength. We, as exiled adults in our lapsed fallen condition, can touch this marginal power of strength. This adds to the consoling power of the story whether or not it has a happy ending – that we have actually witnessed something we've lost. We are reminded of our loss, which is an irony, but at the same time we gain access to something. So even if this is not the childhood we had – most of us were not brave enough not to pray when the teacher tells us to (and certainly my own childhood was passed in absolute terror of all figures of authority, which meant that I was incredibly good and absolutely dead keen never to be found out if I ever did anything wrong) – we can still identify with these magically heroic delinquent figures. An upbeat film of this sort is John Boorman's *Hope and Glory*, in which the children take a completely different view of the war from their parents and teacher, crying out 'Thank you, Hitler!' when their school is bombed. Through them we are able to identify with the dissenting voice.

A fourth aspect of the disjunctions between the child's point of view and ourselves arises because the self-flattery and the consolation involved in all of these things actually amounts to the end of innocence. In most of these kinds of films, the child has moved from the prelapsarian condition to something that nearly matches adult consciousness by the end. That is, of course, another irony: that our condition is, in fact, the only inevitable outcome.

The simple moral landscape of fairy tale, with the victim or innocent at the centre, intensifies the childish atmosphere of such films: good and evil are presented in fairly distinct terms, blame is often apportioned and justice meted out. An absolutely wonderful example of this is when the cruel pastor in Bergman's *Fanny and Alexander* is burnt to death. I for one have never desired someone's vengeance as much as I wanted vengeance on him. The effect of the similar revenge in *Celia*, when she kills Uncle John, is much more ambiguous in comparison – and more shocking.

Many of the childhood point of view films are also about initiation, which often entails some sexual knowledge, and several of these have explicit fairy tale settings: *The Company of Wolves*, *The Magic Toyshop*, *Labyrinth*, directed by Jim Henson (which didn't so much involve sexual knowledge but which nevertheless was about a child growing up through a quest), and, of course, *Celia*. I've been talking about these types of films without actually discussing the sex of the child in question – and I'm using 'sex' advisedly here because the story often shows the development of bodily sexual characteristics into social gender. These tales of initiation are often tales of discovery, tales of adaptation or tales of rebellion. In either case, what happens lays down in a sense the map which is subsequently going to determine that child's later adult movements.

This idea that the child exists as a kind of beyond-sex cipher, a consciousness that is not sexed, relates in a sense to these ideas about the paradise, the innocence, and this tension is present in many of the contemporary treatments of children: that the child is both asexual and sexual at one and the same time. *The Company of Wolves* begins with the pre-pubescent little girl lying in bed dreaming and through these dreams, in which she encounters the wolves and elaborates on stories told to her by her wise old granny, she arrives at some kind of sexual knowledge. While Angela Carter's perversely brilliant stories occasionally suffer slightly in their transferal to the screen, she has made that terrain of initiation (specifically female initiation, female self-discovery of erotic pleasure) very much her own literary territory, and wonderfully so.

II

I'm now going to turn to one of the oldest fairy tales, and, keeping in mind the symbolism of childhood, try to tease out its connections to the work of Jean Vigo. I don't know if Vigo was aware of the tale of *Cupid and Psyche*, but I usually operate on the basis that people don't have to be conscious of the links, the antecedents to their own work, because the mind can be fertilised unconsciously by many things. 'Congener' is a useful term for a theme or motif which is held in common by different people who may not have received or developed it from the same Ur-source; a congener differs from an archetype, however, in that it possesses a cultural character, subject to change and even disappearance, unlike the archetype in the Jungian sense.

In 1933 Vigo made *Zéro de Conduite*, an absolutely emblematic founding-father film of childhood school delinquency. His next film was *L'Atalante*, a romance set on a barge. I think that *L'Atalante* contains much of this founding fairy tale of *Cupid and Psyche*, and I'm going to attempt to develop that.

The story of Cupid and Psyche is included in *The Golden Ass*, written by Apuleius in the 2nd century AD. It tells the tale of how Psyche was beloved by Cupid, the god of love, and consequently incurred the jealousy of his mother Venus who was also very jealous of Psyche's beauty. Psyche loses Cupid after she lights a lamp and the oil falls on his shoulder as he sleeps and wakes him – and she has been forbidden to look at him. This is a very important part of the later development of allegory: the theme that you must not look love

46

in the face. So Psyche sins through her curiosity, and subsequently has to go through many ordeals before finally recovering Cupid in the end, marrying him and having a daughter whom they call Pleasure.

I'm now going to quote from the story, and you will see how absolutely recognisable the fairy tale motifs in it are. Psyche has been homesick and she has gone home to see her sisters:

> It will be wrong for us to hide your danger from you. It is this, that the husband who comes secretly gliding into your bed at night is an enormous snake with widely gaping jaws, a body that could coil around you a dozen times, and a neck swollen with deadly poison. Remember what the Oracle said, that you were destined to marry a savage wild beast. Several of the farmers who go hunting in the woods around this place have met him coming home at nightfall from his feeding ground, and ever so many of the people in the nearest village have seen him swimming across the ford there. They all say that he won't pamper you much longer, and that when your nine months are nearly up he will eat you alive. Apparently his favourite food is a woman far gone in pregnancy.

These are the ugly sisters, of course, turning Cinderella against her beast lover. He is also presented as a kind of fantasy Bluebeard. However, we don't know if Apuleius originated some of these motifs himself (which is extremely unlikely) or if he had received them and integrated them into this story.

What is interesting, in terms of our theme, is that the story of Psyche (the childish heroine who is young and innocent) and of her quest doubles the story of the narrator of *The Golden Ass*. When Apuleius wants to tell a story which will give us the meaning of the larger book he assumes the voice of a female narrator. The story of Cupid and Psyche in the book is told by an old woman to a young woman who has been abducted on her wedding day by bandits. In order to tell his fairy tale, the author sets up an entirely feminine context and atmosphere. He migrates, as a writer, into both the voice of the old woman to tell the story (to her female listener), and he creates a female protagonist whom he calls Psyche – the soul.

Now the word for the soul is, in most languages, feminine. *Anima* is feminine in Latin; indeed, such abstractions very frequently are. The whole tradition of the representation of the soul tends to represent it as a child – the soul in Christian imagery, for example, is almost always represented as a child. I think that two things converge here: the idea of generic humanity (the soul) which is going to enter the world and undergo certain experiences, and the idea of the child as a feminine representation.

What happens in *Cupid and Psyche* is that Psyche, the girl seeker for love, meets love himself. There is a further doubling because Eros – Cupid – is constantly also represented as a winged child, and therefore love and the soul in our tradition share this iconographic attribute of childhood. And, of course, Cupid is in this respect connected to the representation of fairies. We have another strand in the world of the supernatural which is not Christian, nor indeed classical. This is the world of the Celtic supernatural, the 'wee folk', who are also a kind of winged child. I need only remind you of, for instance, Ariel in Shakespeare's *The Tempest*, 'my airy spirit':

> Where the bee sucks, there suck I;
> In a cowslip's bell I lie;
> There I couch when owls do cry.

So this cluster of symbols – this tiny soul, the *animula blanda*, the human seeker, the fantastic supernatural dimension and the eternal energy of love – all are present. As I said, I don't actually adhere to the theory of archetypes, so I'm not suggesting that this sort of thing swims or flies around, like Ariel, in the air. But I do think that there are ways in which our consciousness is constructed and reasons why these symbols are present in our Western tradition.

The genderless child, who touches both spirit and love, is supported by one little scrap of evidence from the history of childhood: that in the past, social gender doesn't seem to have been determined until rather later than we determine it now. Seventeenth-century portraits of children, for example, frequently show boys in the same clothes as their sisters. I recently went to the Victoria and Albert Museum to look at photographs in family albums, and was very struck by an album which had recently been donated to the museum by a man. He had been photographed on his birthday every year by his father, from around 1900 onwards, and in all the photographs his hair was curled in ringlets, he wore a little lace collar, a skirt and little shiny boots. To our eyes you could not tell he was a boy until he reached the age of seven. I once wrote a book about Queen Victoria's watercolours, which consisted mostly of sketches of her children, and again they all wore dresses, regardless of whether they were boys or girls, until a certain age. The specific masculine gender as a prerequisite of the boy child actually comes in rather late in our cultural education.

What is interesting is that the arrival of sexed identity does spell an end to the kind of innocence that I have been talking about, and of the asexuality of the soul which corresponds to some kind of angelic state. In *Zéro de Conduite* it is perhaps surprising that the little boy who looks like a girl, and is teased for it, later emerges as the leader.

48

This is because, in a sense, he has not yet fallen into the social requirements of gender, but rather retains the charismatic capacity attached
almost universally to the androgyne. Yet this kind of thing usually
focuses on the figure of the tomboy, not the girlish boy. The tomboy
is almost invariably the centre of the fantasy which prevents or pushes
back the moment of the Fall. In *My Life as a Dog* there is the little
girl who boxes with the hero, for instance. This is a very common
heroic, attractive type of child in films of childhood.

I want to suggest one of the reasons why so many films (and, indeed,
literature) about initiation focus on girls, and are often made or
written by women: I think that they are feeling somehow this undertow of symbolism, that the soul, the seeker, the psyche, has a feminine
physical constitution before entering adult differentiation. It certainly
seems to be an undertow in Angela Carter's work, and in her interpretations for the screen, in *The Company of Wolves* and *The Magic
Toyshop*. It's also very strong in *Celia* and in the short film *Down to
the Cellar*, directed by Jan Svankmajer, where the child protagonist
experiences established Freudian encounters such as the key and the
shoes eating one another. And in a way it's necessary that this child
be a girl; it would be difficult to imagine that film with a little boy.
There is something in our attitudes that makes it more appropriate
that we witness the arrival of sexual consciousness through the eyes
of a girl child.

There are two films by a woman film-maker which are very interesting in terms of this idea of how the soul becomes a social being. These
are *Le Livre de Marie* and *Mon cher sujet*, by Anne-Marie Miéville,
Godard's partner. *Le Livre de Marie* is rather an ambiguous film. It
is slightly related to *What Maisie Knew* in the sense that there seems
to be some sort of marital quarrel going on in the background between
Marie's parents, and she arrives at some kind of awareness of the
adults' tension. But of course it's called *The Book of Mary* because
it's also a sort of Gospel story, and as it was exhibited with Godard's
version of the Virgin Birth, *Hail Mary*, we consequently experience it
with Gospel overtones and they enhance the enigmatic innocence of
the protagonist.

Mon cher sujet is an exceptionally interesting film, I think, and it
takes much further this idea of child development. It is about a woman
at the centre of five generations of women – she has her mother and
grandmother on one side and her daughter and grandchild on
the other. What is very unusual and original about this film is that
the experience of life (the artistic creation of life, the making of your
life or the being made by your life) is not seen as something which is
only experienced by the child, it is also something the mother experiences. And in psychoanalytic terms this represents a most unusual line

of enquiry. We're not just in the mind of the child, we become both mother and child, because the mother who is at the centre of our consciousness was a child and brings her own knowledge of having been a child to the understanding of her own children. I think Miéville has developed here richly and subtly the multiple point of view that the cinema is capable of in a single protagonist's narrative, while making the important moral point, that innocence cannot be defined without experience. She in effect denies the notion of Fall and shatters the end of childhood as an image of the Fall: her adults are children, too.

DISCUSSION

Duncan Petrie

One thing I am interested in is the distinction between films for children and films about childhood. What is interesting is that you didn't take a negative view of films for children, because it seems to me that in the classic Hollywood vein – the Disney films and things like *ET* – there is a certain embellishment of innocence which is almost a refusal on the part of adults to properly retrace their own childhood. These films play on a myth of innocence which you lose when you become an adult, and I don't think this is a particularly progressive stance to take. Do you have any thoughts on this?

Marina Warner

Well, I must say that some of the Spielberg type of films, which I think are quite entertaining, are nevertheless built on a kind of duplicitous flattery of the child. They usually present the child as knowledgeable and wise in a way that adults are not. There's also another film – Terry Gilliam's *Time Bandits* – where the parents explode, vanish into dust, at the end and we all cheer. That kind of fantasy is often present in the Spielberg school – that parents need to be led by their children. In a way this is a sort of compensatory fairy tale, and it is one of the functions of fairy tale and fantasy to extend compensation. Because basically children have probably never been so powerless as they socially are now, except in certain terms of economic power – called 'pester power' by advertisers. The nuisance value of children has probably risen socially because they are so targeted by commercial interests. We have all had experience of toddlers and children, who are beginning to watch television and to be affected by the ads, pestering their parents in supermarkets and wailing in misery because they have not been given this thing or that thing. At the same time, the conditions of urban life have actually contained the child, and indeed the parents or parent, more than ever before. The car has effectively stopped play outside regulated areas. There is also less free circulation between the generations than there used to be. So the fantasy in these films, like *Back to the Future*, of omnipotent children not only breaking down the barriers of the reality principle, but breaking down all forms of social control which they are normally expected to obey – this is just a compensatory fantasy which flatters them.

Robert Carver

Can I question some of that? Speaking as a film-maker, one of the key groups of people actually buying tickets now are children, teenagers and immediate post-teenagers. And I expect that, to some extent, film-makers – particularly Hollywood film-makers – actually flatter children quite deliberately, coming in on *Back to the Future* and this notion of compensatory roles that children are given. In fact, the children are seen as being much wiser, more competent and perceptive than adults, and I think this is almost a cynical ploy in some cases. You said that children had never been so powerless, and you added, quite correctly, the rider that what they do have now is a substantially economic power. In terms of the cinema this is fairly crucial. It's not just pester power in terms of buying this item in the supermarket, it's pester power for being taken to see this film rather than that film. I would say that children are now a very significant economic force in the cinema. I would also suggest that there is a general reluctance among the adult cinema-going population to accept the Freudian implications in cinema with their own children that they would accept around the table at a dinner party. In other words, middle-class, educated, enlightened people are quite willing to accept that children have some sort of Freudian sexual feelings, but to actually see these represented in fictional children in the cinema is still, I would argue, almost completely unacceptable. So to some extent, the children that we see portrayed in the cinema now are, on the one hand, flattered – super-adults who can do all sorts of things adults can't do – but on the other hand they are almost completely desexualised. We never see childrens' sex play in the cinema or on television. It's almost completely a taboo subject.

Marina Warner

There has been an increasing use of children in stories aimed at children, a new development totally different from the history of children's entertainment. Puss in Boots is not a child, Sleeping Beauty is a young person but she's not actually a child. The age of the protagonists in tales for children has consistently dropped. There is a way in which Narcissism is seen as a key to entertainment, and I think that with that has come the kind of self-censoring manoeuvres you've described. In quite a lot of early fairy tale films, what happens is that very similar material is actually acted by grown-ups, with the effect that it is suitable for children to watch. In the 1925 *Wizard of Oz*, Dorothy (as she does in the book) has two suitors: the two farmhands who become the Tin Man and the Scarecrow. And when she's subsequently transported to Oz, one of the wicked characters who has usurped the true Kingdom of Oz also wants to marry her, and she has to fight him off. By the time we come to the 1939 film, Dorothy's age has dropped to around twelve years of age and she is too young to have any sexual experiences.

Ed Buscombe

I'm a little concerned with what I think is a rather simple economic determinism that seems to be coming through from the speaker at the back [Robert Carver]. The argument, as I understand it, is that, because children now have more spending power, therefore there are more children who are the heroes of popular fiction, including the cinema. But I think that one can find plenty of instances going well back into the early years of this century, and indeed into Victorian times, where children are very much at the centre of the narrative. I suppose a *locus classicus* would be *Peter Pan*, which probably does represent some kind of watershed in terms of fairy stories and the role of children within the narrative.

Marina Warner

And also, very importantly, the asexuality of childhood innocence.

Ed Buscombe

Yes, but I think, certainly going back to my childhood in the late 40s, and what one knows of popular fiction for kids in the 20s and 30s –

the 'Just William' stories, 'The Bash Street Kids', and 'Dennis the Menace' – all of that predates Stephen Spielberg by some fifty years.

Robert Carver

The comics were not usually bought by children, as I remember. But surely there is an economic determinant in that movie-making is a business as well as an art form. All those American films of the child hero variety are tested out by the producers, often over months, with specially invited audiences – children of the age group that the pictures are targeted at – in key demographically typical areas of the United States. Each member of the audience fills in a card after the screening indicating the points they like and the points they dislike in the film; and the film is subsequently re-edited to suit the target-audience taste and prejudices, sometimes as often as ten or twelve times.

Ed Buscombe

All I'm saying is that there's a long history of children's literature, such as the stories my daughter used to read like *Heidi* and *Anne of Green Gables*, which considerably predate that phenomenon of the contemporary cinema.

Marina Warner

I think there is a slight difference between the literature you have touched on and cinema: that quite a lot of those books are really very descriptive of the material conditions of the life those children lived. In a book like *Heidi* there is a realistic evocation – perhaps not altogether truthful, but detailed and knowledgeable – of growing up in Alpine pastures and suchlike. But in a sense it isn't the *What Maisie Knew* syndrome: we are not in a tunnel vision of the child as something out of society, looking at it. So there is a storytelling tradition in literature which actually does tell stories of children's lives, as opposed to using the child's consciousness as a device to say something about adult life.

Gillian Hartnoll

Isn't that the difference between books about children which are essentially addressed to adults, as in *What Maisie Knew*, and children's stories? One of the things which has been said of fairy tales is that they are about children coming to understand the world into which they are growing. And that seems to me to raise some questions about there always being a child protagonist in films addressed to children, because if part of childhood is about growing towards adulthood, then presumably the fairy story, in talking about that transitional phase, is quite important with regard to the child coming to terms with, and having an understanding of, that new stage of life. So that if all the films for children are locked into stories with children as protagonists, it seems to me that that aspect of it is getting lost.

Marina Warner

I agree. I also think that when there are fewer child protagonists, in terms of the engagement of fantasy with the real, the fantasy framework of film gives access to the unsayable or the unwatchable experience; in a way, it's a device to permit this to be said. So it is the act of seeing that is fantastic, rather than what is seen. What is seen is metaphorically presented but is in fact real. It seems to me that this is an aspect of stories like *Donkey Skin*, about a father wanting to marry his daughter. This is a way of telling a story to a child which can reflect the real, can hold up an imaginable danger which cannot be spoken, and that fantasy is about the only way you can do this. Child sexuality is present in both literature and representations, but never as such. But then again, the whole symbolic construct of all art is to do precisely with not having to present things literally.

Nicholas Tucker

It seems to me that a lot of what you are saying applies not so much to children but to anybody on the screen who hasn't the same competence as we do, and consequently engages very much our anxiety, sympathy and compassion. But they don't necessarily have to be children. For example, the novelist Nina Bawden wrote a book early on in her career called *Devil by the Sea*, where a child sees a murder happen, and the murderer knows the child has witnessed the murder and is out to get the child, but no one will listen to the child. However, Bawden's last book is called *Family Money* and this time it is an old lady who sees a murder. Her wits are beginning to go. She doesn't make total sense so no one believes her. But the murderer knows, and she is on her own. So you have a similar situation but with an old woman rather than a child.

54

Marina Warner

That's a very perceptive point. But actually it goes beyond the cinema and has its roots in the history of childhood entertainment. Because if you think of the figure of Mother Goose and how she is presented in childhood literature, you get a familiar refraction of the childhood condition in old age, and especially the female old-age condition. Mother Goose is introduced as the proverbial storyteller. She existed as a phrase in French, but Perrault subsequently used her in the title of his 1697 collection, *Mother Goose Tales*, and then she passed into absolutely common parlance. What Perrault is doing there is a perfect analogy of what happens in films, and also reflects exactly what Apuleius is doing in his *Cupid and Psyche* tale. The adult whose consciousness actually directs the narrative pretends to be a child, but the actual persona that he presents as the author is an old woman. So the old woman and the child converge in the viewpoint of the piece. Perrault actually said that his son, who was about fourteen at the time, had written the *Mother Goose Tales*, but the teller was Mother Goose. So you get that doubling. In the same way, in *The Golden Ass* the story of Cupid and Psyche, which is the embedded fairy tale in the book, is given to the voice of the old woman to speak, as I was saying. So I think that you are right, that in a way these two figures stand at the confines of the social. It will be interesting to see, now that we have so many homeless old men, if the marginal will become occupied also by the figure of the prophetic man. But certainly I think that the idea of the crone, the witch, the old woman who is sometimes discounted because she is the most vulnerable figure in the history of society, is one confine, one pole, and that the child is at the other pole.

Tana Wollen

I want to make a point about *Celia* which is about identification. It seems to me that one of the most interesting things about *Celia* is that it shifts the point of identification from the girl to the mother, who for three-quarters of the film is actually this kind of marginal, rather ignorant figure. And what the film seems to be about is not so much a loss of innocence, but rather this act of repression that has to take place. The father represents one kind of repression: 'Behave yourself. No, you can't have a rabbit. Don't go into that room again.' Whereas the mother's initial marginality, her 'wishy-washiness', leads to an ending in which she has to repress from the whole family history the act of revenge Celia carried out on Uncle John. And this final act of repression has to take place, paradoxically, in order to prolong Celia's childhood.

Marina Warner

You are right, because I think that the last scene of *Celia* (the hanging of the scapegoat) isn't a successful scene, and the film would have been better ending with that moment when the mother represses, as you describe, the killing of Uncle John and conspires silently with her daughter.

Tana Wollen

Except that, as the audience, you are shifted from identifying with Celia suddenly to identifying with the mother: what would you do in a situation like that? And it's as though the repression won't work because bubbling up through Celia somehow is this tainted innocence.

Marina Warner

And the mother enacts that process quite literally when she holds the white sheet over the bruise (caused by the recoil of the rifle against Celia's shoulder) so that the doctor won't notice it. Her gesture is symbolic of exactly what you are saying. The film does have an unsettling resolution, but I'm not sure that doesn't intensify its power.

Tana Wollen

I'd seen *Celia* before, but I had forgotten what Celia does to Uncle John. I'd completely erased it, I had in fact repressed it. And I was talking to a female friend of mine and she had done exactly the same – completely forgotten what Celia does to her uncle. And so perhaps as an adult you want both of these points of identification: with Celia and with the mother, and yet the actual act has to be erased. So I think this relates back to the point about what texts allow you to identify.

Marina Warner

The point about *Mon cher sujet* – it's interesting that it translated as 'My Favourite Subject' but is also, in a sense, 'My Dear Subject' or 'My Dear Self', the kind of revolving self inside the inter-generational pattern – was inspired by a paper written by a friend of mine called Susan Rubin Suleiman. Her paper is on motherhood, specifically on mothers who write. She draws attention to the tendency to view the drama of creation, the drama of individuation and of differentiation, from the point of view of a child looking at an adult, at the mother. She turns this around, to propose that in certain texts, adults are being made by their children, rather than the expected other way round. Mothers who write are rather a new phenomenon, she points out, in that many of the women writers in the past didn't have children. In a sense they're rebuilding their lives from the point when they start writing (which can be relatively late) so that the child becomes a symbol of their own career. I don't know if that is true for women film-makers – how much there's an actual exchange with their own lives, or if they're mainly remembering their own childhoods rather than experiences of raising children and identifying with them.

Nicholas Tucker

I'm surprised that you described the girl in *The Nasty Girl* as a child. I always saw her as an adult. Once again I can't help feeling that this innocence you refer to isn't a quality necessarily of childhood, it's a general quality we attach to people not taken seriously by others. The 'nasty girl' ends up a married woman but is still alienated by society because no one will listen to her or tell her the truth. And yet one is as concerned for her innocence in the face of this cynicism as one would for a character ten years younger.

Marina Warner

I think the question of curiosity is interesting here. One of the ways in which the child transgresses is through not knowing what the limits are, and one of the ways this is demonstrated is through acts of curiosity. This is particularly appropriate in cinema because of the connection between curiosity and seeing. There's the good child, as in *Witness*, who sees, but then there are the bad children who also see something that they shouldn't have seen and sometimes act upon it in ways which can do harm. The notion of curiosity is obviously the guiding motive of the character in *The Nasty Girl* and, indeed, is the dynamic of Psyche's endless problems.

Philip Wickham

One thing I'm interested in is the opposite to this idea of the child as an innocent who will be tainted. There are many examples in which the child is a corrupt thing which has not been civilised, has not learned that people shouldn't be cruel to each other, like *Lord of the Flies*, *Highway to Jamaica* or *The Bad Seed*.

Nicholas Tucker

The Bad Seed is a story about a murderous criminal child and innocent adults. The adults don't believe the child could have committed the murder because they can't think that any child would be that awful. In fact, one can find the theme of innocence and experience in all art, particularly so when children are there, but also when adults are involved too. For every innocent child you can probably find a guilty one; for every over-knowing adult you can find an innocent one. It's just an eternal polarity in all stories, and on the theme of fairy tales we must always remember that it is not always the good and innocent who win the day. There is also the trickster-hero, a worthless type who wins the prize through deception and mental agility. He is an example of the triumph of knowingness over innocence, another popular theme in fairy tales.

Marina Warner

The reason I haven't mentioned the trickster is because the trickster, who tends to be a male figure, isn't such a recurrent figure in popular culture today. One of the reasons for that is to do with our attitudes to language and cinema. The trickster is a riddler, someone who may sometimes perform conjuring tricks but often deceives. The paradigm of the trickster is Odysseus in the story of Polyphemus. He tells the Cyclops that his name is 'No one'. And so when Polyphemus has the stake through his eye and is dying, his comrades ask 'Who hurt you,' and he shouts in reply, 'No one hurt me' – Odysseus's verbal dexterity overcomes the giant.

Tana Wollen

I would like to consider the horror genre and think about the nasty child in Katherine Bigelow's *Near Dark*, which is a brutally violent but very gripping film about modern-day vampires who travel around America in a camper truck which is covered with aluminium foil during the day to stop them dissolving. The young boy, who is around the age of nine, is just completely violent and evil. Interestingly, he is played by the same actor who plays the young sidekick of Crispin Glover in *River's Edge*. It's almost as if this kind of genre portrays an America which is beyond any redemption. Perhaps it's precisely because of the fact that children are playing these parts which signifies this. It's not really about the loss of innocence, because its almost as if there never was any innocence, certainly none that we can remember.

Robert Carver

Can I pose two antitheses and ask which you think is more accurate? Do you think film-makers tend to use children as a dramatic device in the same way that Montesquieu used his Persian diplomats in Paris – that is, allowing one to have an oblique view of the adult world – or do you think that there is a specific generic type of child in cinema that is related to themes and cultural patterns that has nothing whatever to do with adults in films?

An example of the former is *Whistle down the Wind*, with Hayley Mills who plays the child who discovers the tramp. All the children take literally what they've heard in church – that Jesus came down to save Man. And in the tramp they think they've discovered Jesus. That doesn't make sense unless we step back and see the children as a dramatic device used by the film-maker to point out the hypocrisies of the adult world – that we as adults know that Jesus isn't going to come down but the children take that to be literally true. And this seems to be a recurrent pattern in film-making.

My second antithesis is an attempt to encapsulate what I think your central thesis is: that there is something special and unique in the way that children are presented, that in some way they are separated from dramatic representations of adults in film. And I should like to suggest that children in films are not in fact particularly different from other types of characters. Other powerless characters have been mentioned, such as old ladies, who are used as oblique points by which the protagonists' unbelief in their perception is seen.

Marina Warner

I think that children are still a much more prevalent and powerful symbol than other marginal figures, though I take the point that other marginal figures can be used in a similar way, as witnesses. And there is a sense in which the relation to the centre needs to be defined from the outside. It's quite possibly a continual dynamic in art.

Robert Carver

But the centre's power holds. If a strong male patriarchal figure holds the power then the wife or grandmother can be seen as oblique critical figures. *Lord of the Flies*, for example, is the adult world with the adults taken out. And its interesting that the children simply take up dominant/passive/oblique roles.

Gillian Hartnoll

What I should like to suggest in relation to this idea of children and other marginal figures is that everybody has been a child, but not everybody has been an old woman or a simpleton or whatever. So that may be the reason why perhaps children have a particular force.

Man

I wonder if some of the things mentioned wouldn't be around issues of power and powerlessness, and then across that, questions of realism and fantasy. I'm thinking of things like *An Angel at my Table*, from Janet Frame's books, or Bill Douglas's film *My Childhood*, where within a realist mode what you are looking at is either children who, in a sense, early on get some perception of what they are or what they want to be, or how they disagree with the rules of their society. You then follow through the conflicts – which is often a case of surviving what are almost incomprehensible experiences – they have in order to somehow or other sustain their identity. *My Brilliant Career* is another case in point. Now, I would expect these are rather different from the fairy tale fantasy film.

Marina Warner

Although I actually think that's related to the central proposition of the Bettelheim book, which is that the more savage the ordeals the child has to undergo, the more the wicked stepmothers eat the hearts of children, the more capable it renders a child to cope with the horrors of life. *Salaam Bombay* is another example of how very distressing events in a child's life might have the therapeutic effect of the audience which Bettelheim describes. In a sense, hope is extended by seeing a picture about something worse than we experience ourselves, and this relates closely to the use of fantasy in film. The story might appear to be realist but for us it works on a different level.

Robert Carver

Do you think there is a problem of actually knowing too much, seeing too much and receiving too much: and that we all, as a very self-conscious, post-Freudian generation, tend to do just this? That one hundred years ago people reading the original brutal Grimms' fairy tales didn't actually see all these Freudian things about incest; and that consequently the message or the warning was passed on in an unconscious way that we can no longer do?

Marina Warner

No, I don't think so. I think they were terribly aware. The history of the Grimms' transmission is one which has been rather well recorded, and they were extremely aware of the pedagogical, didactic enterprise; they re-edited the tales accordingly, while at the same time claiming that they were taking down the *Volksprach* exactly as spoken from the unadulterated voice of the people. They actually put the stories through seven editions.

Robert Carver

The Grimms did, but what about the people they claimed to have received the tales from – the ordinary people out in the forests of Bavaria and Saxony? Do you think they were self-conscious and aware of the Freudian implications?

Marina Warner

I don't think one need be aware of the Freudian implications to be worried about what the material contains. There are hundreds of factors which affect the storytelling scene before it reaches print, one of which is the fact that there was a mixed audience. The process of socialising and moulding becomes totally different because they aren't being recited in a schoolroom or indeed in a nursery. These stories are being told to grown-ups by grown-ups. There may be the occasional child present as well, but children are not in the consciousness of the teller in the way that they are in the printed versions later.

WOMEN AGAINST WOMEN IN THE OLD WIVES' TALE

Internal BFI Seminar, 26 February 1992

Marina Warner

The idea that 'the beastly' represents the childish rings an interesting variation in the fairy tale tradition. The Beast's state of enchantment always denotes the less than human. But in the 18th century this was the result of an evil spell which had reduced the Beast to his lower animal state and deprived him of speech as well as of comeliness. Cocteau in *La Belle et la bête* is, of course, faithful to this, with his Beast (Jean Marais) inarticulately grunting and growling and frightening Beauty in the process. In Disney's animated version of *Beauty and the Beast*, the Minotaur-style Beast is a captive of childishness. He wants to escape and grow up. So it is his immaturity and self-indulgence which represent the less than human. However, he will eventually arrive at full human 'personhood' – marked by sexuality, love and language – through Beauty's attentions and her growing love for him. Whereas in the 18th century women were trying to turn men into civilised people rather than savages, by the 1990s they are helping men to grow up from acting like little boys. It's a development which rather perfectly synchronises with changing attitudes both towards and between the sexes.

When the less than human shades into the not human in the fairy tale, different rules govern male and female figures. The male creature, either transformed by an evil spell or created with fiendish ingenuity, tends to be animal-like and is characterised by shagginess, grunting, preternatural strength and size: conventional masculinity magnified. His caress is an assault, his desire destroys. The manufactured maiden, by contrast, magnifies femininity in its most girlish and virginal mode. She is often beautiful, wears white, she speaks in a light, squeaky voice (if she speaks at all) and she dances prettily for her maker.

Both these figures appear in an interesting group of films which I have came across while doing the research for these seminars. These films feature automata, puppets and artefacts which come to life. This

63

is a theme with which the cinema feels a great affinity because it's something the cinema can achieve rather successfully, after all: making inanimate objects come to life. The most brilliant example is, of course, *Frankenstein*. The creature in the Frankenstein myth learns, or attempts to learn, language, symbolism, the ways of society, in exactly the same way as the fairy tales which communicate this kind of fantasy attempt to make children learn language and symbolism on the way to adapting themselves to society. But what's unusual about *Frankenstein* in some ways is that it is about a man. Very frequently this type of story or film concentrates on turning a doll into a woman, that is, creating a woman, and it goes back to the creation of Eve and the creation of Pandora. Indeed, in his famous essay on the uncanny, Freud wrote a long essay on *The Sandman*, E. T. A. Hoffman's nineteenth-century story about a doll-maker who brings dolls to life. There have been several serious, even tragic interpretations of the story, like the ballet *Coppelia* by Delibes, which was filmed, in full sugary style, as *Dr Coppelius* in the 50s. In these versions, the doll really does prove to be the ideal which the human falls short of. The most surrealist and powerful, however, was created by Michael Powell (with Robert Helpmann and Moira Shearer as the Doctor and his Doll) in one of the macabre and magical episodes of *The Tales of Hoffman*. And Angela Carter picked up this theme in *The Magic Toyshop*: she has her children in a toyshop where the dolls come to life.

But I want to concentrate here on two films which deal with the theme. One is *Die Puppe*, the 1919 Lubitsch comedy which is quite a subversive and witty film in which a little boy accidentally destroys a luscious doll his father has made for a client. The client doesn't want a real woman for a bride because they are so troublesome, but instead wants an automaton who will, of course, do what he wants. So the doll-maker creates an absolutely exquisite doll, using his daughter as his model. And so, when the little boy breaks the doll by mistake – by winding it too hard – the daughter has to take the place of the doll and marry the client. The film then begins to disengage him from his misogyny: the daughter goes on pretending she is a doll and plays a lot of tricks on him, gradually tricking him into humanity. So it has a happy ending.

Die Puppe relates in some ways to *The Bride of Frankenstein*, directed in 1935 by James Whale. Beauty personified, played by Elsa Lanchester, is created by Frankenstein and his wonderfully sinister collaborator Dr Pretorius, who himself specialises in making puppets and is shown bottling his shrunken creations and gloating over them as they perform tricks for him. At the end of the film the bride, the crowning wonder of the pair's science, comes to life in a magnificent shower of sparks and great technological spectacle, only to reject her desired partner, the creature. She wants only her maker, Dr Franken-stein, and the spurned creature responds by blowing them all up – a beast unredeemed, unrestored to the human.

In Lubitsch, in a comic vein, the soul who has been fashioned and changed and has entered into the social sphere, through marriage, manages to redeem her beast – following the romantic tendency of this kind of tale. But in *The Bride of Frankenstein*, she actually refuses the role: in a sense, she refuses to end childhood, to grow up into a woman, which the Beauty/Bride/Puppe accepts when she leaves her father's house and adapts to her husband's.

So while the enchanted male becomes a Beast and escape from this form is what renders him more human or more lovable, the enchanted female is a doll and escape from her prescribed state often entails her becoming less desirable, less conforming to her maker's or lover's wishes. Frankenstein and Pretorius make a woman to be a perfect mate for Boris Karloff's creature, but she brings about the tragic destruction of everything, including the laboratory tower, because when she opens her mouth for the first time she fails to utter the acquiescent, gentle accommodations of a bride, but rather rejects the creature with a scream. This image of a woman's speech threatening the stability of the world into which she's brought is a recurring one, in this kind of tale, as well as in romantic fiction on the screen.

Last week I saw for the first time *The Magic Toyshop*, adapted by Angela Carter from her own novel. It was rather extraordinary – rather uncanny, indeed, and very moving – to sit and watch this film so soon after she had died and to discover how autobiographical it must be. It's a study of a young girl growing up, and director David Wheatley cast a young actress (Caroline Milmoe) who looks very like what the young Angela Carter must have looked like.

This theme which I have been talking about – the idea of a man who wishes to master the feminine by actually creating it according to his desire – is developed in *The Magic Toyshop*. The man takes the form of a wicked stepfather: the malignant puppet-maker who is the owner of the magic toyshop and the creator of the magic toys. He attempts to turn the heroine into his creature and subject her to his sexual fantasies. He creates the tableau of Leda and the Swan, in which his alter ego (manipulated by him at the end of the strings) is the huge swan Jove, the overpowering, priapic god, who knocks the child-swan to the ground. But ultimately he fails to work his will on her in the way that he has on his wife. The contrast between the child and his wife (her ethereally beautiful stepmother) is that one speaks and one cannot. The girl cries out against the assault of the swan, symbolising her rejection of this sexual power. But the wife, on the

The Magic Toyshop (David Wheatley, 1986)

other hand, wears a silver torque around her neck, which has also been made by the puppet-maker, and which is so tight she can only cough when she tries to speak.

What is interesting is that when Freud analysed Hoffman's story *The Sandman* (a version of the same folk tale which informs *The Magic Toyshop* and *Die Puppe*) in his essay on the uncanny, he saw it as a parable about the male castration complex, because when the hero falls in love with the doll and cannot possess her fully, he imagines his own eyes have been put out. But in *The Magic Toyshop*, the nub of the tale is not the castration anxiety of the male lover, or even the potency of the swan/Jove/puppet-master figure at all, but rather the muteness of the puppet-woman and how that can be overcome. And throughout the film – which I think is more integrated than *The Company of Wolves* – the issue remains the conflict between silence and speech, silence and music-making, silence and storytelling.

Now, when the Beast in *Beauty and the Beast* tales comes to speech it poses no threat to the given order. In contrast, speech for the emerging adult female is fraught with social taboos and restraints. This theme of the danger of female speech goes back a long way in storytelling and mythology, and I'm particularly interested in how persistent such notions are in current literary and cinematic fictions.

I should like to quote from the story of the first manufactured maiden, the first woman made in the image of man's desire: the Greek myth of the making of Pandora. It's a very ancient story, but it was written down by Hesiod in two of his poems. I'll quote from *Works and Days*:

> He [Zeus] told Hephaistos Zeus quickly to mix earth
> And water, and to put in it a voice
> And human power to move, to make a face
> Like an immortal goddess, and to shape
> The lovely figure of a virgin girl.

He does so, and then the gods and goddesses gradually come, adorn her and give her skills:

> Grey-eyed Athena made her robes and belt,
> Divine Seduction and the Graces gave
> Her golden necklaces, and for her head
> The Seasons wove spring flowers into a crown.
> Hermes the messenger put in her breast
> Lies and persuasive words and cunning ways;
> The herald of the gods then named the girl
> Pandora, for the gifts which all the gods
> Had given her, was the ruin of mankind.

> The deep and total trap was now complete.

Pandora goes on to open the casket, as you know, in which are imprisoned all the ills of the world. The Greek Eve brings about the fall of humanity largely through her curiosity.

So in that first, fundamental myth of the manufactured maiden, we have this emphasis from the start on cunning and snare, seduction of both beauty and voice, lies and curiosity. And, of course, there are parallels with the Judaeo–Christian myth of the creation of the first woman, with Eve.

Laura Mulvey has written an essay on Godard's film *Hail Mary*, about the Virgin, and addresses this question of how to represent female activity and female speech. She writes:

I have argued recently for a female spectatorship which would replace the visual pleasure focused on fetishised femininity and replace this with the pleasure of curiosity. Curiosity (of course a dynamic of the action) undercuts the belief system and generates a desire to see into forbidden spaces and mysteries. Curiosity has perhaps been associated with women precisely because woman is comparatively inured from the anxiety the female body can produce.

She goes on to say that curiosity is, of course, the sign of the fallen woman: of Eve after the apple, of Pandora who opens the box, and of Psyche, too, who, towards the end of her story, is sent to Hades by Venus to fetch back from the Underworld a box with the secret of Beauty inside it. She, too, can't resist the temptation, even though she has been forbidden to look, and she opens it and is cast into deep sleep. Mulvey continues:

While curiosity is a compulsive desire to see and to know and investigate, fetishism is born out of a refusal to see, fixing instead on a substitute construction. Under this complex turning away, of covering over, closing the eyes to understanding, the female body is bound to remain an enigma and a threat.

So Mulvey is actually offering the idea of the questor, of the inquisitive, curious heroine who sees and investigates as the antidote to the fetishising spectacle of woman on film. I think it would be very interesting to think of the child as this active principle who is constantly challenging the spectacle that is set before us in the cinema as well. Maybe then one could make a more positive characterisation of the child as viewpoint, using the child as this kind of investigator who throws expectations and challenges what one would normally expect to see.

I think this is a most acute insight into why the thrust of curiosity and of the questioning voice can be seen as threatening by men who see it as issuing from a female body which they find alluring, and how this danger is lessened in the case of the female receiver of the same female voice.

If you think back to *The Nasty Girl*, you see there a questing child growing into a questing woman, an investigator who reports and then brings back the news of what she's learnt. But, again, she threatens the stability, the fixity of the world where she is speaking. It can also be true of the male questor (men can also destabilise by questioning and investigating) but I think there is a tendency that a nasty girl looks nastier when she is doing the same thing, that she is indeed a nasty girl.

However, the human faculty of speech and the pursuit of knowledge are signs of the civilisation that the transformation of the Beast in a sense demands. So it is in the very act of civilised behaviour that women are seen as dangerous. One of the things about this particular double bind in which the female sex is caught is that it has an extraordinary persistent history, and as long as I have been working I've come across passages in which this is expressed. The fathers of the Church rant and rave about it, medieval schoolmasters pick it up, the *Roman de la Rose* is full of it, and so on. This is an absolute rock against which the foot stumbles in the history of the perception of woman: the danger of the woman's tongue.

Now, the tenacity of discourse is in itself a kind of myth which becomes severed from actual historical circumstances to persist as a transcendental story everyone knows. In his book on medieval misogyny, Howard Bloch writes about Christine de Pisan who, in the 15th century, lamented the violence done to women in Christian writing and literature. After quoting her replies to male detractors of the female, Bloch comments:

> Leaving aside for the moment the unknowable affective element of anti-feminism as well as the social status of actual women at any given moment, *misogyny is a way of speaking about, as distinct from doing something to, women* [emphasis added]. Though speech can be a form of social action and even social practice, or at least its ideological component, such a distinction between words and deeds where relations between the genders are concerned is the necessary foundation of a dialectical, historically informed, political understanding of women, an understanding which otherwise would remain hopelessly enmeshed in the literalism of false ideology – a literalism that risks taking gender difference rather than the oppressive exercise of power by either sex for the true historical cause of social injustice.

This idea that misogyny is a speech act relates it to misogyny as a story, which I think is something one can hold on to. In the movies we have speech acts about women in a very suggestive form, because films are themselves speech acts as well as image acts. And the speech acts of the characters, when they are women, can reinforce from within the attitudes (prejudiced or not) that are circulating in society and that in a sense form images themselves. When you see a speaking woman articulating speech acts which are misogynistic, they receive a kind of warranty from within.

In fairy tale films actions and spells go together. The spells advance the story. Wishes, curses, demands, conditions, prohibitions, chants, incantations, riddles, songs: these are the stuff of fairy tale and they provide the actual narrative structure of the stories, or propel them on. The oral tradition, naturally enough, encloses a very strong belief in the power of the spoken word to bind and to loose – 'The tongue has no teeth but a deeper bite' is a proverb from Spain which is apt in this context.

The relation of women to the spoken word is highly marked in fairy tales, and the ambiguous disquiet registered about what Hesiod calls 'women's lies and persuasive words and cunning ways' informs the reception of figures like fairies and godmothers, and has trickled into the representations of talking women and enchantresses on film. To put it rather crudely, it's a rule of thumb in fairy tales today that the less a female character speaks the nicer she tends to be. And, I would argue, this can also be applied to film. Concomitantly, the softer the women speak the nicer they are. Take Lear's Cordelia for example: 'Her voice was ever soft,/ Gentle, and low; an excellent thing in woman.'

Ruth Bottigheimer has written a very good study of the Grimms' fairy tales entitled *Bad Girls and Bold Boys*, in which she marks the disparity between what the Grimms thought was considered valuable and creditable for boys on the one hand, and for girls on the other. She includes an appendix in which she has tabulated the speeches from the different characters in fairy tales such as *Rapunzel*, *Hansel and Gretel*, *Cinderella*, *Little Briar Rose* (the Grimms' *Sleeping Beauty*) and *Rumpelstiltskin*. This graph demonstrates that the 'good' girl asks something only once and speaks about ten times on average. The witch and wicked stepmother figures, on the other hand, are always making demands and are the most garrulous characters in the stories by far.

Even more significantly, by tabulating different editions of the Grimms' stories, Bottigheimer found that 'good girls' tend to speak less and less as the Grimms refined the material. So, for example, when they first took down the story of *Cinderella*, she protested that she wanted to go to the ball, spoke out against her fate and asked not to have to do the household tasks that the Ugly Sisters set her. But by the third edition, the Grimms found this rather difficult and edited her speeches so that she simply accepted that she wasn't going to the ball and applied herself to the household tasks without protestation.

It would be interesting to apply Bottigheimer's system to the Disney versions of *Snow White* and *Cinderella* and see what actually happens in terms of their speech patterns. As I remember, Cinderella is very soft-spoken with a high pitched, little-girl kind of voice, while the Ugly Sisters are often vituperative, always screeching at her and commanding her to do things. This imbalance of speech would seem to reflect Bottigheimer's findings.

70

In terms of representation, the witch figure doesn't just speak more than the heroine, she is, of course, usually a certain kind of woman: ugly and often old. The cinema's investment in female beauty also creates an affinity with fairy tale, where beauty usually represents the side we should be on, and ugliness represents the enemy. However, the old and haggard crone storyteller or gossip is also a crucial figure in the actual telling of stories. So there is a crossing of these two things: on the one hand the good voice of the storyteller, and on the other the wicked voice of the witch, who resembles her in some way within the story.

The place of ugly old women in misogynistic thought has a very long history. There is a French print from 1660 which depicts Lustucru, the '*médécin céphalique*', or 'skull doctor', hard at work. With the help of a hammer and anvil he is forging anew the heads of women who have been brought to him by their menfolk (chiefly their husbands, but in some cases their fathers) for a once-over that will turn them into proper wives and women. The inscription on the bottom of the print relates how the doctor learned the secrets of his trade in Madagascar, probably a sly reference to head-hunters. Then it describes the women's offences: they are shrewish, loud-mouthed, angry, mad, devilish, annoying and obstinate. One inscription reads: 'Great man, by your care almost all our wives are now well behaved and give us peace' – that is, they keep quiet. It continues by saying that they cannot offer adequate thanks for his great feat, except to honour his name for ever more. In the centre of the print, on the anvil itself, the inscription reads: '*Touche fort sur la bouche; elle a méchante langue*' ('Strike hard on her mouth, she has a wicked tongue'); there is also a little figure who has no head at all, and underneath it says: 'This is much the best way for a woman to be.'

This print is one of several variations which appeared around the same time, and there are Italian and German versions in existence. It was the brainchild, appropriately enough, of a priest, and it was inspired by the controversy over the bluestockings in the Paris salons. These were a seventeenth-century group of female writers and poets called the '*précieuses*', many of whom interestingly enough used fairy tale as a form in which to express their ideas and conflicts. A prolonged and intense quarrel was provoked by the ambitions of these women, who wished to be the intellectual equals and companions of men rather than their mistresses or their wives. They also fought an interesting battle against arranged marriages.

The example of Lustucru's imagined powers gives a new twist to an ancient theme in folklore. The recycling of wives when their menfolk are tired of them develops the darkly humorous theme of the mill of youth, or the mill of wives, which also circulated in print form in late medieval and early modern Europe: the example I am describing is a Danish version from the 19th century, but I've also seen it in books from France and Germany. The undesirable wives are brought to the mill by their husbands because they are superannuated, in need of rejuvenation. They're fed into the mill (they come in with sticks and hooked noses, haggard and toothless) to be ground and whittled, and re-emerge whole and young, vigorous and loving. Curiously enough, their husbands haven't suffered the same effects of old age.

The difference between these two examples of popular culture isn't as great as it may first appear. The association between a woman's face and figure and her tongue lies at the heart of a male quest for the desirable partner. To look fair and to speak fair are linked feminine virtues. Following from that, to look foul and to speak foul is ugly. Indeed, the ugliness of Lustucru's victims lies principally in their tongues, because female old age represented a violation of the proper purpose and this carried implications beyond the physical state into wider prescriptions of femininity. Indeed, one of the things that occurred during the conflict over the *précieuses* in Paris was that they were accused by men of being ugly old maids, therefore asking for the things they did. This was, of course, a very easy way of attacking them for demanding greater social equality.

Traditions of rhetoric and iconography enabled the image of the crone to express other matters beyond the simple decline of physical health or strength. They had turned the outer form of the old woman into an allegory of denatured woman, which could be extended to include unwifely transgressions: of disobedience, of opinionatedness, of anger, of lack of compliance. The virtue Obedience, for instance, traditionally holds her fingers to her lips in medieval iconography. When the object of desire talked back, therefore, she lost her desirability. The penalty for this, the ready-to-hand representative imagery of female undesirability, was the appearance of physical decay – the outer mark of unwomanliness, of being against the prescribed purpose God had decreed for woman. In the Judaeo–Christian tradition, the Christian Fathers' view of the place of woman in the world was, broadly speaking, procreation. Otherwise, as Aquinas said, 'Why would God have made a helpmeet who was female?' – a male helpmeet in the Garden would have been much better in every other respect for Adam. So childbearing became the *raison d'être*, the only excuse for the seductiveness and desirability of women. A famous text putting this point of view comes from St Paul's First Epistle to Timothy, in which he says, 'A woman ought not to speak. Nevertheless, she will be saved by childbearing.' So there you have the crux of the idea that the seductress in every woman is only redeemed by procreation.

Consequently, a theme develops that takes the infertile woman who has passed the age of childbearing as representing in some fundamental way a transgression against the purpose of her sex, and in that transgression against the natural God-given order she can then serve to represent other pejorative and repulsive or repugnant aberrations. Hence the connections between beauty and virtue on the one hand, and ugliness and vice on the other. And one has to remember that this still persists as a very pernicious aspect of our combined moral and aesthetic judgments.

The criterion of desirability so often rules allegories and ethics – the worse the vice, the more undesirable the chosen appearance for the image – that for the particularly dangerous area of sexuality and its linked sins, like vanity, the old woman emerges as the most fitting repellent image. There is a Dutch engraving entitled 'Vanity' which is taken from a painting called *The Old Procuress at the Toilet Table*, by Bernardo Strozzi. This makes an important shift between representing a social profession (in a fanciful way, no doubt) of the old procuress, but making it an allegory of a perceived female vice, vanity. Indeed, allegories of vice are often hard to notice: they can look like naturalistic documentation such as a woman at her dressing-table. They are, however, morally loaded documents about the sin and folly of vanity.

The allegorical traditional mingles with, and influences, conventions of naturalistic representation and narrative. In seventeenth-century Dutch painting, for example, the figure of the procuress often appears, and is represented as toothless, chap-fallen and scraggy. The Dutch historian Lotte Van Der Pol has combed the Amsterdam archives for the confessions of prostitutes and their madams in the 17th century – the Dutch have the best archives of this kind of material in Europe – because prostitution has been legal in the Netherlands for so long. She has pieced together an extraordinary, and often surprising, picture of the conditions in which prostitutes worked. One of the things she has discovered is that the average age of the madams was between thirty and thirty-five, because the moment the younger women could leave the job of actually doing the prostitution and instead run the business and the girls themselves, they would do it. So even if you allow for differences in life expectancy between now and the 17th century, the women in the paintings and engravings are certainly only in their thirties – yet they are represented as ancient crones in order to put across the message of their moral character.

The long tradition of allegorical vice goes back to the Graeco–Roman imagery of strife, anger and envy, and has modified the pictorial language of sexual transgression. When the Dutch genre painters turned to the scenes of city life, the language available to them for communicating the identity of the procuress was particularly limited: it was provided by the classical and medieval vocabulary of sensual sin. They therefore returned to the hag as a cautionary tale about the penalties of lust. Allegory has a long reach, deep into the seemingly most realistic forms of representation – and these include film.

Since classical times, the hag has been reviled. But the hag who doesn't know herself to be a hag and instead preens and coquettes and pretends to be seductive like a young woman comes in for special abuse. And the allegorical hag's sins are not bodied forth only by the impairments and disfigurements of age – the tendency develops of representing her transgression through the sins of her mouth, especially the evils of her tongue. Indeed, vices like anger and envy are often associated with noise and cursing. An example from recent popular culture of these iconographic characteristics of vices coming down through the medieval tradition is the character of Zelda in the Gerry Anderson TV serial *Terrahawks*, who is a coarse-spoken, hag-like figure of dangerous and powerful evil.

The principal sin with which the tongue is connected is lust, which goes back to Eve and Pandora. Indeed, at the time of the Fall the serpent's seduction depends on talk. Paul was making this connection when he prescribed silence for women and then went on to blame Eve for the Fall. In medieval representations, the Devil at his work of tempting Eve to sin sometimes mirrors her own face. He often looks like a woman and is also sometimes represented with wrinkled female breasts – the breasts of an old woman which have lost what is perceived to be their true purpose, nursing.

A cardinal text for the associated evils of lust, woman's aberrant sexuality in old age, and female talk, was provided by the First Epistle to Timothy which I quoted earlier. There, Paul goes on to list the varieties of improper talk in which women indulge, and in the list he uses the term 'old wives' tale'. At the very beginning of the Christian era old women were linked with idle stories, with bawdy talk and with tittle-tattle. This brings us to the heart of the fairy tale.

One of the earliest secular books of tales attributed to women is called *Les Evangiles des Quenouilles* (*The Gospel of Distaves*), which first appeared around 1475 and was translated into English by Caxton's follower Wynkyn de Worde in 1507. It relates what the author, a male scribe, describes as a typical session of women's gossiping and consultation among themselves, of their storytelling; he says the women invited him to write down what they said. The text belongs, generally speaking, to the tradition of gossiping of which tale-telling is a branch. Numerous references in other works, from sermons to popular plays, provide evidence that this book was widely known.

An Italian, Straparola, who had collected stories also described them as being told in a circle of women. At this stage in medieval storytelling these kinds of stories often contained a lot of obscenity, as well as quite harsh, tough material. Consequently, Straparola was summoned before the inquisition for indecency, where he defended himself by claiming that it wasn't his fault, he had only taken down what he'd heard the women say. This excuse is a very common one and was also used in *Les Evangiles des Quenouilles*, where the writer informs us from the start that he has been called in as a mere scribe to record the wit and wisdom of the gathering, which is exchanged over a series of six days (the traditional Hexameron). The questions that the women ask themselves are practical and frequently erotic. The old wives give remedies for impotence, for wife-beating, for unwanted babies; they interpret dreams and omens and fortunes; they recommend love potions; and they give advice in the handling and understanding of animals and their behaviour. In other words, all the tasks connected with natural processes which was traditionally then the domain of midwives, layers-out and, of course, witches. The whole text is presented in a mock-scholarly facetious style, and the glosses are offered by the attendant ladies. Many of the remarks are very salacious and the female commentators are given lurid names: Bellotte la Cornue (Bella the Horned One), Transie d'Amour (Pierced by Love), Isabelle de la Crête Rouge (Isabella with the Red Crest), Noir Trou (Black Hole) and so on.

The *Gospel of Distaves* sends out conflicting messages, which is actually quite characteristic of the whole genre of 'old wives' tales'. But it's clear the spindle talk gathers together women of different classes and contains dangerous secrets about love and the government of men that transgress against rational perception. The male scribe, by picturing such erotic conspiracies among women alone, denies any male responsibility for current fantasies about sex by ascribing them to women. At the end he refuses the offer of an erotic reward of one of the women and ends with the warning that 'what's written in these gospels demonstrates the frailty of those who gossip together like this'.

So *Les Evangiles des Quenouilles* is an example of bawdy medieval misogyny which contains a series of speech acts but which conforms to conventional wisdom when it lumps all women together, whatever their walk of life, and scorns them as foolish, irrational or frail, especially where talk and fantasy are concerned. As the decades go by, attacks on the material in these mock gospels grows more fierce and less humorous. The veracity of its contents is disputed – in other words, the remedies that it offers are said to be trash – but the presumption that women believed and practised such beliefs passes unchallenged. The association of old women in this way, from Medea's nurse to Juliet's, with talk and persuasion and erotic love (vice), does need to be properly studied because there is an extraordinary amount of popular materials condemning women for their gossip and their tale-telling. An English print, for instance, from the 17th century, depicts different tasks which women traditionally undertake – at the laundry, in the kitchen, drawing water, and so on. At the top of the print it reads, 'Tittle-tattle: several branches of gossiping.' And the verses in the print condemn the kind of gossip and conversation that goes on when women are engaged in these tasks. There is a French variant, also a popular print, which again represents traditional female pursuits – feeding, cooking, shelling, spinning, laying-out, delivering babies – and at the top it reads 'Le caquet des femmes' ('The cackling of women'), and fights are breaking out in different places on account of this troublesome chatter.

A good woman, on the other hand, was considered to be a silent woman. She wore a padlock on her mouth (literally, in some representations) and when she went to the fountain she didn't tittle-tattle or cackle.

I want to try to relate all this to the figure of the wicked stepmother and the malignant types of woman in fairy tale. As you will all be aware, the good mother often dies before the story begins, in tales such as *Cinderella*, *Snow White* and *Rapunzel*. She is typically replaced by a screaming hag; in fact, these beloved classic tales teem with such figures of female evil. In one seventeenth-century Italian version, Cinderella is landed with no less than six ugly sisters by her new stepmother. In fairy stories, monsters in female shape outnumber ogres, giants and beasts, and we are often more frightened by the figure of the witch than by any other.

The phrase 'old wives' tale' was already pejorative when Apuleius, in *The Golden Ass*, used it on the lips of his crone. She said: 'I'm going to tell you an old wives' tale to cheer you up.' The pejorative slur has remained in the very act of authenticating the folk wisdom, the ancestral voice present in the stories. Old women are invoked as the tellers who were carrying out an ancient tradition. But the term 'old wives' tale' carries a double connotation (and in that respect it relates to the power of the witch) such that it is constantly teetering on some ambiguous knife edge between positive and negative. George Cruickshank's frontispiece to the first collection of the Grimms' fairy tales in English is a typical nineteenth-century representation of the old woman storyteller by the hearth: wizened, gnarled, hunched, poor, needing to walk with a stick. An 'old wives' tale' is still, in English, an ambiguous phrase: it means 'a piece of nonsense', 'a tissue of error', 'an ancient act of deception', 'idle talk'; but it also implies (as fairy tale does) fantasy, escapism, invention, and the consolations of romance.

In his review of Calvino's collection of folk tales, John Updike made the connection with film and television and how they function in society. He wrote of fairy tales: 'Their inner glint, their old life, is escapism. They were the television and pornography of their day, the life-lightening trash of preliterate peoples.'

Angela Carter also spun this connection between the soap opera *Dynasty* and the old wives' tale, between the role of the storyteller in the village or by the hearth and the role of television now. She calls fairy tales 'the literature of the poor', the oral storytelling which binds society together in collective myths.

But as I have said, there can be a Utopian impulse behind all of this; it can be a way of telling an alternative story, of sifting right and wrong according to a different voice, and a voice that is perhaps disregarded, discredited or neglected. It's interesting that the old woman, the most vulnerable figure in the household in a sense, and one of the most traditionally reviled figures, is the carrier of this particular voice. In times of crisis, of fragmentation and violence, romancing can serve a richer purpose than escapism. The critic Gillian Beer has written, in a wonderful essay on romance which goes back to this medieval form: 'Romance, being absorbed with the ideal, always has an element of prophecy. It remakes the world in the image of desire.'

I think this is why there has been such an extraordinary resurgence of interest in fantasy and romance, which is reflected in films like *The Fisher King*. It seems to me significant that Terry Gilliam has moved from the science fiction fantasy of *Brazil* into a specifically medieval romance form of fairy tale for *The Fisher King*.

The possibilities of romance thus include the possibility of altering inherited prejudices and stock figures; but consciousness of their structure is to some extent necessary in order to do this.

The historical roots of the vile, tyrannical and evil-tongued woman are obscured today. The Wicked Stepmother has become a popular archetype, beyond the realms of Walt Disney. I recently saw on television the film adaptation of Graham Greene's novel *The Confidential Agent*, where a treacherous Spanish landlady pushes the young skivvy, a Cinderella figure, out of the window and murders her. The actress was dressed, and her hair was done, in exactly the image of the fairy tale bad fairy. The wicked witch in *The Wizard of Oz* also inherited these physical characteristics as well as the vituperative tongue. Anjelica Huston has made her own raven-haired and aquiline beauty a strong suit in modern variations, like *The Grifters*, as well as in Nicholas Roeg's parody of the genre *The Witches*, written by Roald Dahl.

But when history falls away from the subject we are left with speech acts that go on being pronounced and reaffirming themselves in an endless cycle. The archetype is really only a hollow metaphor, which through usage has lost its connections to contemporary understanding and experience, and goes on perpetuating false consciousness. An analogy would be the metaphor of sunrise or sunset, familiar visual images which fail to represent altogether the present state of knowledge about the movement of the sun or the relation of the planet to it. It's a speech act which in a sense perpetuates a lie.

One of the reasons why I liked, in a very different way, the comic film *Miranda*, produced by Betty Box, and *The Fisher King*, is that both films shatter the mould of the sour and tough-speaking woman. Miranda is a mermaid, a seductive fantasy figure, who speaks her own desires quite openly and sometimes shockingly – swallowing live fish, for instance, when she's taken to see the sea lions at the zoo. But the phallic imagery remains light, and Miranda herself a positive enchantress. In *The Fisher King*, which reveals the relationship between the apocalypse and fairy tale in the contemporary moment, there is an interesting reinterpretation of the tongue-lashing seductress. Mercedes Reuhl acts the role of the hero's lover with an uncompromising strength of character and temperament, and yet she doesn't fall into the kind of self-caricature that actresses are so often led to creating on screen. Terry Gilliam has written there a conventional romance in which the female principal saves the knights both from themselves and from their demons. But the sheer particularity of the character Mercedes Reuhl created prevented her part from becoming a mere idealised pawn in a buddy movie about male redemption.

In Greece, the women of the Thesmophoria rituals kept their thoughts and deeds to themselves – men were not admitted to hear or witness what they were doing. They understood the risks involved in speaking female matters to a mixed audience. The open circulation of women's experiences, hostilities and sufferings in the fairy tale and other materials has certainly given hostages to fortune, handed ammunition to the very figures, the princes, who often caused the fatal rivalry in the first place. Women were trapped on the fine, reverse-barbed hooks of allegiances and interests on which, like fish, they became more and more ensnared the more they attempted to pull away. And in a sense they, and we, are still caught on these invisible lines.

DISCUSSION

Nicholas Tucker

Sartre's description in his autobiography *Les Mots* of his mother reading to him as a small child is interesting. He sits down with her and then says that his mother appeared to shut her eyes when she looked down at the book and started to read. When she got to the character of the witch he was convinced she had turned into a witch and he longed for it to be over, when she'd go back to being his mother again. It struck me, thinking about this when you were talking about the role of the narrator, that as an adult one is often dragooned into reading these stories, even when it's not entirely something you wanted to do. An extra element to your theme, therefore, could be this controlled aggression an adult sometimes feels towards a child who demands that a story be read, the way such aggression is sometimes experienced in the stories themselves.

Marina Warner

I think that that corroborates the idea that there is some competition for authority going on for the storyteller. But at times the stories have been simply learned by heart, have been handed down, and are not renewed by the storytellers. So one can't say that in each storyteller's mind it is instrumental in developing control over the household.

Cary Bazalgette

It's interesting that we tend to refer to the tradition of storytelling as an oral tradition, because presumably it was also a tradition of performance. You have these images of the old woman sitting there and presumably just talking, but one imagines that stories would have been semi-performed. I don't mean standing up and actually performing the drama, but there would have been changes of voice, expression, deliberate comedy, song and frightening of the children.

Marina Warner

I'm afraid the people who collected these stories were not at all interested in such details. It's a real problem in the anthropologists' and fieldworkers' collection of material, because how can they remain invisible and not affect the actual performance of the ritual or the telling of the tale? After I had given a similar paper about this in Holland an anthropologist sent me a very interesting paper he had written. He was working on a tribe very much organised along matrilineal lines and he had just collected a story from a man when a woman from the tribe came up to him and told him her version of the same story. He subsequently broke these two versions down into segments and did an extremely interesting analysis of the different agendas and interests at work and how they reveal themselves very strongly in the same story. The female storyteller was tremendously interested in the female character's resistance to an arranged marriage, whereas the male storyteller was interested in how eventually she was married to somebody. There was a complete difference of emphasis. So the idea of identification with the protagonist was quite strong, as opposed to the thesis I was trying to develop that the storyteller might have a cause of her own to serve than just identifying with the protagonist.

Cary Bazalgette

An interesting example of alternative versions in circulation is a story you haven't mentioned – the story of *Goldilocks*. There are two beginnings to that story. One version begins 'Once upon a time there was a little girl called Goldilocks', while the other starts with 'Once upon a time there were three bears'. And I think I'm right in saying that in the history of the story Goldilocks has become a more problematic and ambivalent figure. She has become more a pretty little girl whereas she was originally much more ugly and destructive.

Marina Warner

I should have talked about it because it's also a good example of female curiosity, and I should imagine that its history first deals out a punishment to Goldilocks for being so daring and independent and enterprising, and then gradually that shifts and becomes slightly different. I know the Walter Crane version in which the Mother Bear is terribly fierce and she says that she is going to 'skin' Goldilocks for the Little Bear's supper. This is an example of how bears have changed, they have become much more cuddly.

Gillian Hartnoll

I wonder if the virulence of some of the images of gossiping women you talked about is related to the kind of virulence with which black people were regarded – the creation of horrific images which justifies dominance and enables repression to continue?

Marina Warner

Yes. There's an extraordinary overlap with similar black material. When there were few black people in Europe you don't get them targeted overtly; who you do get targeted are, of course, the Jews. The similarity of discourse and caricature there is really remarkable. If you think of the physiognomy, straight away there is an absolute overlap between the grotesque caricature of female old age and the representation, for example, of the mockers of Christ at the Crucifixion in serious Christian imagery. I've done a lot of work on medieval storytelling and there's a lot of overt anti-Semitism in material which contains overtly anti-women tales. That's why I tried to say that what happens when the wicked stepmother is taken out of the historical context and becomes this 'other' – this amalgamation of images of otherness – you then have that perniciousness working in exactly the same way as you do with any racist representation.

Gillian Hartnoll

One thing I was wondering about was the way in which we seem to have stuck with this same set of stories and representations, and how that relates to the loss of storytelling as a direct tradition. The modifications which you talked about seem to have gone, because the number of storytellers has dried up and so consequently there is a tendency to revert to the tales that are in existence and tell them as they are.

Nicholas Tucker

An interesting alternative model of the witch is the Lorelei, the mermaid, the siren, who attracts principally by her sexuality and her singing. But the one thing you don't do in the children's books is to bring in sexuality as a weapon. So one reason for the virulence of the traditional representation of the witch as an old hag is that she's the most desexualised woman you can possibly imagine – toothless, bent and hideous. I always imagine that is a way out for illustrators and storytellers from not having to confront children with anything to do with sexuality at all.

Marina Warner

Except that Disney's films are full of sexuality. And the wicked step-mother in *Snow White*, when she looks in the mirror she's meant to be the most beautiful.

Nicholas Tucker

But most children are more frightened by her as a younger woman than they are by her as a witch because she has that classic 'bad woman' beauty? It's not a sexual image, it's a power image.

Tana Wollen

Cruella de Ville in *One Hundred and One Dalmatians* is a very frightening figure. She's also got all the characteristics of beauty. But it's a kind of beauty gone wrong, there is a sense of allure which is actually what is quite frightening about her.

Christine James

Picking up on the point about the Lorelei and the idea of the alluring but sweet-singing woman who draws sailors to their death, this made me think of Disney's *Snow White*. She is terribly sweet and she sings when she is cleaning the dwarves' house. I wonder where women making that kind of noise fits in with the idea of women's talk as noise?

Marina Warner

One of the earliest places that you hear women's voices without quotation marks round them is in opera. As soon as opera is actually sung by women, as soon as women actually get on to the stage, there is this sudden reprieve for the female voice which is also an acknowledgement of its sincerity, that it no longer lies. But then the whole idea of the female performer's sincerity is rather different from the male's. The idea of the Janis Joplin or the Billie Holliday figure – these are people who we are led to believe are pouring out their inner being in their voices. But this image may be changing – Madonna certainly isn't doing that.

82

The siren is a Janus-faced figure in the sense that she sings from the soul but is also a seductress who cheats and deceives. And in a way that whole dichotomy is compounded by the continuing argument about stories. There is a very good novel called *A Servant's Tale*, by Paula Fox, which is about a woman who comes from one of the Caribbean islands to work as a maid in New York to rather rich bourgeois women. She remembers her grandmother telling stories and how she asked her, 'What's the difference between a story and a lie?', to which the grandmother replied, 'A story seeks to uncover the truth. A lie seeks to hide it.' But of course this is an ongoing problem – what is fiction's status with regard to truth? So in that sense 'the Siren's Song' can be construed either as a story which uncovers the greater inner truth as she pours out her soul, or as the deceptive lie. I don't think this can be solved and it's one of the dynamics that bears on the storytelling tradition in different media.

Cary Bazalgette

Isn't that always the way with very enduring images or metaphors – they have a tension within them they can't resolve? Isn't that partly why they are so enduring? I think that what is so interesting about the figure of Margaret Thatcher, you had people from whatever political position talking about Thatcher, describing Thatcher, drawing pictures of Thatcher and so on, and what sort of ideas and myths were available to be drawn on there.

Marina Warner

I think she did get a lot of mileage out of her femaleness and I think she possibly got a lot of mileage out of misogyny, in a paradoxical way, in that she wasn't treated equally by her cabinet because they were frightened of her. Of course, it's partly her own individual personality, but there are male myths that increased her own terrifying persona. I took part in a valedictory programme *The Late Show* made about Margaret Thatcher, and I was rather annoyed at the way it was later edited. I felt the questioning was very leading in that the hostility was in some way celebratory. I tried to make a number of points about the vulnerability of her position and how she had been discarded by men when she no longer served the storyline function they wanted. There were many ways in which I think she set herself up as a kind of Aunt Sally to be knocked down when the moment came because she was so heavily symbolised. Anyway, most of this was edited out in order to maintain the image of this Marie-Antoinette figure who rode roughshod over the people, which in a way just continues the mystique.

Julia Noakes

It's interesting comparing a film like *The Little Mermaid* – which has the mermaid who can't speak representing the good woman, and the evil witch representing the bad woman – with melodramas from the 30s and 40s in which the female protagonists are much less clearly marked and more ambiguous, and which consequently allow a subversive reading which women can take from them. I'm thinking here about films like *Stella Dallas*.

Marina Warner

I certainly think that the search for a large audience has worked against films which challenge assumptions in this way. And interestingly enough, considering that I'm so interested in speech and in women's language, the silent films were very innovative in some of their expressions and representations of women's lives because they don't have this problem. They start with silence so they don't have to face the question of when a woman speaks out she is somehow transgressing against the given order. When you come to *The Little Mermaid* you have the good woman who is silent, so if you have an active-tongued woman in the same film how do you characterise her? I love the smart, fast-talking woman like Rosalind Russell in *My Girl Friday* and I regret that these kinds of films don't seem to get made any more.

CAT PERSONAE

Lewton, Sequelhood, Superimposition

John O. Thompson

One striking difference between a certain *image* of the fairy tale and the feature film is that the former is told or read outside market circumstances, in the most crucial non-market enclave of life, the family, while the latter is brought into being as an experience to be bought. Of course, the economics of storytelling are not, and have never been, as simple as the image suggests; in traditional societies the storyteller may well be paid, and the cultural producers of fairy tale texts and images, from Perrault to Sendak, have operated as authors and artists within the regime of the market. But the child listening to someone (mother, father, older sibling, aunt, babysitter, co-opted visitor) telling or reading her a story does not pay.

Sequelhood, therefore, does not enter into the fairy tale reception experience. The child, having been told the *Little Red Riding Hood* story, or the *Cinderella* story, or the *Beauty and the Beast* story, does not as a result of that satisfactory experience call for *Little Red Riding Hood 2*, or *Daughter of Cinderella*, or *Return To the Beast*.[1]

Val Lewton[2] did not make *The Curse of the Cat People* as a children's film (it could hardly have been sold as such, being a product of what was set up as a horror unit within RKO), but he did make it as a film about childhood. He did not make a film which was about any Curse of the Cat People, but he certainly made a film which is a sequel to *Cat People*. He made a film to which the question of fairy tale narrative, of 'the uses of enchantment', is overtly central, in a way in which it is not in the prequel film.[3] The later film thereby opens something up in the earlier film which would otherwise not be visible.

My first reaction to *The Curse of the Cat People* was that it constituted the most amazingly, and movingly, *reparative* sequel to any grim fiction that could be imagined.

In *Cat People*, Irena believes that her ethnic identity (Serbian, as it happens) includes membership in a race of cat-people, and that sexual

85

contact will cause her to turn into a panther. Her husband, Oliver, while sympathetic, considers this to be a delusive belief, and psychiatry is indicated, in the suave form of Dr Judd. Oliver's anxieties about the marriage bring him together with a workmate, Alice. Irena's jealousy of Alice turns out to be able to trigger the transformation, leading to the film's great scenes of menace. But the catastrophe is finally triggered by Dr Judd's sexual advances towards Irena, with the two 'un-Americans' (Dr Judd as played by Tom Conway speaks with an English, George-Sanders-type accent)[4] responsible for each other's deaths. This leaves the way clear for Oliver and Alice to become a proper couple.

In *The Curse of the Cat People* Oliver and Alice, as proper couple, have produced a daughter, Amy, who is sensitive and lonely. Oliver in particular is worried because he believes her to be confusing fantasy with reality; it also bothers him that she doesn't play with the other children, that she doesn't have 'friends'. Amy is given a ring when she ventures into an Old Dark House inhabited by an old lady, Julia Farren, and her daughter Barbara. Julia Farren is a former actress, now physically infirm and in the grip of a delusive belief, namely that Barbara is not her daughter but an impostor. Encouraged by Edward, the Jamaican servant, to believe that the ring is a wishing ring, Amy

The Curse of the Cat People (Robert Wise, 1944)

wishes upon it: her wish is to have a friend. The friend who appears is the ghost of Irena.

Amy is happy with her friend, but her father becomes all the more anxious about her (despite reassurance from both Alice and Miss Callaghan, Amy's teacher). Irena decides it is time to withdraw from Amy's life; this however precipitates Amy's stealing out of her room (to which she has been sent by her father as a punishment) into the cold, snowy night in pursuit of her departed friend. After wandering lost in the woods, she reaches the Farren house, where Julia lets her in. However, things have deteriorated between mother and daughter, with Barbara, jealous of her mother's affection for Amy, having spoken of killing the child if she returns to the house. Taking this threat seriously, Julia tries to find a place for Amy to hide; but in trying to ascend the stairs to the hiding-place with Amy, Julia collapses and dies. Barbara confronts Amy, whom she accuses of having stolen even her mother's last moments, and the encounter does seem potentially murderous; but Barbara 'is disarmed by the child's innocence just as Oliver arrives with the police', as Siegel puts it.[5] The film ends with Amy and a chastened Oliver both 'seeing' Irena in the garden.

The ways in which *The Curse of the Cat People* 'repairs' *Cat People* include the following:

- Most importantly, of course, Irena is allowed to return.
- She returns as 'friend' to the daughter she could never have. (She is allowed to remain not-mother in the process.)
- The realm from which she returns is presented as one of great peace. *Cat People*'s poignancy in dramatising the misery of Irena's existence is thus 'answered'.
- Amy is clearly Irena's successor as unhappy protagonist, in being afflicted with dangerous 'fancies', registered as such by Oliver. But whereas Irena's supernatural belief was a murderous one (I may turn into an animal that kills), Amy's is that animals themselves can be her friends. She slaps the face of the unfortunate little boy who, in catching her a butterfly, kills it.
- The 'right to fantasy' is affirmed in *The Curse of the Cat People* indefatigably, with Oliver the only character who gives Amy a hard time over her fancies (the other children are not shown as particularly beastly towards Amy except in the understandable context of the birthday-party débâcle[6]). Notable here are the female voices of both Alice and Miss Callaghan, the latter speaking as teacher from the position of the expert. Miss Callaghan is the reply to Dr Judd. What makes the *Cat People* material tragic, of course, is that the *fantastique* in which Irena is involved is irreducibly malign: either it is 'all in her mind', in which case she really does have a problem, or she truly is a

cat-person, in which case her existence is unhealably miserable; the film opts for the latter alternative. Another way to put this is that Amy is never in any danger of *turning into* anything or of believing she is in danger of so doing.

- *The Curse of the Cat People* 'desexualises' its troubles, thereby lowering the ante of unhappiness. (What is at stake is not sexual love but friendship.)

- *The Curse of the Cat People* goes to striking lengths to defuse danger or unhappiness around Amy, even though the film is 'about' Amy being unhappy or in peril. We think Amy is being punished for slapping the little boy; in fact, her parents and her teacher are having a most sympathetic conversation about her. We think the birthday-party disaster will lead simply to unhappiness; in fact, the family provides her with a perfectly satisfactory birthday experience. We think in the Old Dark House someone dangerous may lurk; in fact, Julia is welcoming to the child. We think Julia may nevertheless scare Amy by telling her *The Legend of Sleepy Hollow* with its headless horseman, but Edward is there to break the spell and take her home. We might think that Irena may mean Amy no good,[7] but this narrative option is not taken up; indeed, as we shall see, Irena 'saves' Amy at the one moment in the film in which she is in danger. Even here, family and police arrive in time to have averted any danger from Barbara. A real puzzle about the film, in fact, is how it maintains narrative tension in the face of all this reassurance.

- Irena 'saves' Amy: this is the mysterious climax of the film, which is possibly (like Ethan's, 'Let's go home, Debbie,' in *The Searchers*) a high cinematic moment which is too sublime to be wholly satisfactorily realised, and is none the worse for that. The phrase from Siegel quoted above in the plot summary is clearly inadequate, but he expands this to a more reasonable version later in his treatment: 'as [Barbara] menaces Amy, the child summons Irena to her aid by muttering "My friend . . . !", an appeal which calms Barbara's fury'.[8] This gets some of what is happening, but not all of it.

Julia dies, sobbing, after saying, 'I can't do it!' Amy tries to rouse her: 'Mrs Farren! Mrs Farren!' The child draws back from the corpse (showing not much fright at death as such), and is faced with two inanimately frightening things, a lace curtain blowing in the wind (departure of soul?), and a dimming of the lights because of the storm. The music gets scary. Then Amy sees Barbara in an extreme high-angle shot (motivated by the staircase), and the scene continues via a succession of shots giving Amy's point of view (POV) of the frightening face of Barbara and Barbara's POV of the frightened face of Amy, as Barbara ascends (she must have been in the basement). There is a shot of the dead mother from Barbara's POV. Barbara: 'Even my mother's last moments you've stolen from me. Come here.' Amy: 'Daddy!' She shrinks back as Barbara advances. Barbara: 'Come here.' Amy then appeals, not to Daddy, but to Irena: 'My friend? My friend!' (The intonational difference is between a wondering-whether-to-invoke and an invoking cry.) Barbara continues to advance (though her expression changes very slightly, as though registering some puzzlement as to what the little girl is saying). Then the uncanny thing happens: over Barbara's image Irena's is superimposed, so that it is now Irena standing in front of Amy, looking sterner than we have seen her but still with a little smile. Certainly the sight inspires confidence in Amy, who now *advances* to Barbara, saying for a third time, in (mis?) recognition and in wonder, 'My friend!' We get a high-angle shot of Amy walking into Barbara's arms, and a very striking close-up of Amy's hair in the clutches of Barbara's murderous-looking hands. Another, final, 'My friend!' (Amy having no sense now of threat, only of peace); just before this, Barbara's face changes slightly; after it, the hands unclench, the music continues changing away from pure threat, the pattern of shot—reverse-shot is interrupted with shots of the two characters together in profile, Amy embracing Barbara, her head at the level of Barbara's breasts. Barbara looks down at the little girl, her face is shown to soften, then the lights come back up and the noir lighting of Barbara is replaced for a single shot by full lighting, simultaneously with a 'redemptive' musical swell. But Barbara's closeness to Amy is short-lived: the rescue party are seen arriving through the open front door, Barbara retreats, and the Amy—Oliver reunion is accomplished.[9]

I want to return later to what is involved in Irena's 'intervention' here, but her agency in preserving Amy at this juncture is crucial to the film's reparative project.

• Irena does not even leave Amy's life, as she proposes doing when Amy is disciplined for lying. Instead, there is a sense in which she ends the film by being 'there' for Oliver too.[10] The Irena—Oliver relationship, which, for all the gentle satire against Oliver's ordinariness which the films mount, has never ceased to be mourned within them, is thereby ultimately re-established.[11]

Reparation enough, and more. And yet . . .

The effect of the *genre shift* between *Cat People* and *The Curse of the Cat People* is actually violent, even if the direction of the shift is 'peace'. It is easier to see this if one imagines the films reversed in order: after Film 1, a tender and sensitive film about childhood, comes Film 2, in which the comforter and protector is revealed to be a figure of horror.[12] The elaborate game that Lewton played with RKO in terms of being given 'horror titles' ('successfully audience-tested' so 'highly exploitable', in the vocabulary of Charles Koerner, RKO head of production), to which he could respond as creatively, sensitively, and subversively as he liked,[13] is not without its aggressivity. Even if 'Lewton . . . tried to persuade the studio to change [the sequel's] title to *Amy and Her Friend*',[14] we may ask whether such a title change would not have sacrificed a *gesture* which is integral to the ('marketing-perverse') force of the sequelhood enterprise.

One can easily collect from Joel Siegel's biographical treatment of Lewton elements which seem 'relevant' to the two films:

- Lewton really did under certain circumstances have a fear of cats, which he considered to have 'atavistic' roots.[15]
- Lewton's wife Ruth, picking up on this ('He had a folk fear – an atavistic kind of fear of something going way, way back. Of course, he knew better – he was a very intellectual man and not a superstitious person – and so he was both frightened and fascinated by his fear'), associated this with childhood experience. 'Maybe the source of it all can be traced back to the fairy tales told him by his Russian peasant nurse. The old nurse, like many others of her calling, used to control her charges by frightening them half to death. She was strongly aided by the Russian fairy tale tradition which makes the Brothers Grimm seem like very tame stuff.'[16]
- Lewton had a Russian nurse, having been born in Yalta. His mother, Nina, married one 'Maximilian, with his love of gambling and beautiful women'; she left this man when Lewton was two, and 'resumed her family name [Leventon], never again using or mentioning her husband's surname'.[17]
- His mother's sister was an actress. She performed under the name of Alla Nazimova. She had established herself on Broadway by 1906 'in productions of *Hedda Gabler* and *A Doll's House*'.[18] This was the year in which Nina left Maximilian, travelling to Berlin. 'In May 1909 the Leventons emigrated to America . . . where, at Nazimova's suggestion, the name was anglicised to Lewton'.[19]
- 'By 1916 Nazimova was making silent films in New York and managed to get Nina a job as a reader in the Metro New York's story department'.[20] Nina became head of the story department, and in 1928 'got her son a job writing publicity for M-G-M in New York . . . . [She] trained her son in story analysis and synopsis-writing.'[21] This job led on to a writing career; but it was again Nina who put Lewton forward in 1933 for a script assignment for David Selznick ('a Russian-born writer who could do a script of *Taras Bulba*'), which led to Lewton's employment as a Selznick 'Man Friday', which in turn put him in a position to be made the RKO offer.[22]
- The Lewtons had a daughter in 1930. 'It was a difficult delivery which endangered Ruth's life. Lewton was forced to give a direct

transfusion to save her.'[23] Lewton had, it turned out, a very difficult relationship with his daughter: he was, uncharacteristically in terms of his other relationships, to her a demanding and unsympathetic father. She was named Nina.

• Lewton was extremely uncomfortable with physical contact. He 'could not stand being touched or patted on the back'; 'It is extremely difficult for me to even shake hands with people,' he once said.[24]

• *The Curse of the Cat People*, in all its Washington Irving Americanness (Terrytown), is set very close to where Lewton grew up, in Port Chester, NY; the house there (Nazimova's) was called 'Who-Torok', Russian for 'Little Farm'.[25] Verna De Mots, Lewton's secretary, 'in his campaign to Russianise everyone around him . . . [was] renamed Vernushka'.[26] Tom Conway, as Dr Judd in *Cat People*, was 'Russian-born'.[27] (The Lewton days at RKO happen, of course, to coincide with America and Russia being wartime allies.)

The general sense of sequelhood is that the sequel betrays the original. Commercially motivated (or, 'hypercommercially' motivated: one would not want to pretend that originals are not themselves designed to be marketed, that is, designed to be *seen*), the sequel repeats, dilutes, coarsens. How could one *want* a *Psycho 2*? (Imagine a *Vertigo 2*!) To want a *Psycho 2*, as a viewer, is nevertheless not so strange: it is to desire to get back to what was earlier pleasurable, either as repetition or as a carrying-forward.

Lewton's game with the bosses involved 'telling them stories' about what he was going to produce, and then generating something else, which (the great gambling pay-off) then *made as much money* as the crude expected thing could have made. *The Curse of the Cat People* turns the 'telling stories' screw one twist tighter: the unexpectedly successful 'something else', rather than being properly followed-up (as per the story told to the bosses, and duly conveyed by them to the luckless publicity department), is in turn followed by a film which fails to repeat, which takes 'dilution' to the absurd extreme of cancelling horror almost utterly, which 'refines' its original (so that *The Curse of the Cat People* must be one of the most gentle films ever made), and which establishes itself in that most unlikely of sequel positions, that of metatext, 'reparatory' commentary.

But it is in this last role that *The Curse of the Cat People*, once again, turns out to be an excessive or perverse text, in that the *point being made* in commentary on *Cat People* remains elusive. Which brings me, at last, to Marina Warner's reflections.

Warner brings out fascinatingly the way in which women as tale-tellers, given the misogyny of all cultures and the (greater or lesser) difficulty which all ex-infants, female as well as male, have with one side of their memories of earliest dependency, become the focus for fear and hatred. Lewton's enterprise overall is remarkable for its denial, or indeed its chosen refusal, of this thematic. Yet the prequel and the sequel do dramatise fear of storytelling. (Though they do so as, of course, Tales of Fear – which is to say, 'fear overcome'.)

Julia is *scary* for Amy (but Amy can handle the fear, and feels happy with being with the old woman), whereas Irena's folk tale scares herself, and then (weakly) Oliver, (powerfully) Alice, (eventually) Dr Judd, and (shot by shot) us. The fear, diegetically, is beyond defusing in *Cat People*, which makes it the horror film that it is. But the fear is also embodied in the two films by a single actress, Elizabeth Russell. Her screen presence constitutes a powerful *hinge* between the two films. In *Cat People* she plays, briefly and unforgettably, someone from the 'old country' who 'recognises' Irena as caught up in the fantastic–tragic story. On the 'is this delusion or is this real?' question, she gives important, though not decisive, testimony in favour of the latter option. Then, in *The Curse of the Cat People*, she re-emerges as Barbara, the rejected, murderous 'real' daughter (as opposed to Amy as Julia's 'daughter of choice') of the crazed, witchlike, generous, comforting storyteller figure whose craziness consists quite simply in *denying* that Barbara is her daughter.

Reconciling Amy with Barbara 'answers' the Cat Woman (as the *Cat People* credits name Elizabeth Russell) versus Irena bit of the earlier story. But what kind of answer is this?

Mothers, or nurses, tell the stories. It is part of the contract that the child who listens is not caught up in the stories except metaphorically: your situation may be *like* that of Cinderella or Rapunzel or Beauty, but you are not doomed to live within those fictions literally. A worry might be, nevertheless, that you might have to inhabit a tale. Irena in *Cat People* embodies that worry. This echoes the register of psychoanalysis: the infant who listens and thereby moves into speech, and the child who listens further, *is* caught up in a tale, the family story. This can, at its worst, result in something as blocking, albeit non-supernatural, as the nightmare Irena experiences. What is more likely is that the child will face (or the adult will remember having faced) a dilemma less absolute but still spoken-to by this story. (A wide variety of audience members can thereby feel spoken-to by the film.)

The tale, the folk tale, is something that you (Val Lewton) want to tell, in the teeth of the (deracinated, uncultured, philistine) bosses; it is also something whose telling is only worth the telling if the scariness of believing it is made part of the rendering, just as the scariness of first hearing it remains something fundamental to you, to your ability to narrate at all.

A move to metatext here will involve narrativising the storyteller, and possibly doing so, along the lines Warner explores, via the character of the crone or witch – though this will be handled very gently and (at least at first sight) very tastefully.

In *The Curse of the Cat People* the storyteller is supportive to the child Amy, but at the expense of her 'real child' Barbara who is the grown-up carer for the storyteller. Julia, indeed, has a somewhat impoverished narrative repertoire: she can tell *The Legend of Sleepy Hollow* (which Amy can just as well be told at school, the film's opening makes clear, even if she has not yet been), and she can tell about her own past acting glories. She can also tell Amy that Barbara is an impostor, is murderous. Barbara is not an impostor but she is, to a degree never fully specified in the film, dangerous; certainly scary; and her reason for being so is Julia's rejection. If Julia as storyteller can make Amy pleasurably frightened, Julia as deluded person, as unloving mother, leads Amy into the arena of real fear.

The confrontation between Amy and Barbara is resolved by a metaphorical move, a seeing-as: Amy's seeing Barbara as her friend, as Irena. Now Irena comes from a story which Amy is never told. Amy uses the enchantment of Irena to provide imaginary friendship, and the imagination turns out to have survival value in the crisis because it allows Amy to say the words which unlock reciprocity between her and Barbara. The final delicacy of *The Curse of the Cat People* lies in just how fragile this support is allowed to remain. It is mirrored in Oliver's final affectionate mendacious preparedness to say he sees Irena when he has no intention of looking. A fiction, a metaphor, has allowed Amy really to see Barbara as Irena, and this allows for a pact, a co-existence, to replace the murderous rivalry for the mother's love which has threatened the little girl. But the mother's love really has been withdrawn from Barbara, and this is not forgotten at the climax. The visual superimposition of Irena over Barbara[28] operates narratively as a redemptive trigger, but this visual trope is, *through sequelhood*, the superimposition of the tragic Cat Person on the Cat Woman who called Irena back to bear the burden of her intolerable fiction. Will Amy ever be told that story?

Notes

1. There is a strong tradition of *seriality* within the 'children's lit.' field, and not only at the Enid Blyton end of the market: the adventures of Dorothy in Oz and of Dr Doolittle both unfolded over a massive number of volumes, and the (good 'left') names of Nesbitt and Ransome come to mind too. Here we are certainly faced with a commodity logic (children,

or parents, buy the next book in the series because the earlier books have 'worked'), but I would argue that such series operate through a different dynamic than that of the sequel. To shift genres: Agatha Christie's Miss Marple or Marjorie Allingham's Mr Campion or Colin Dexter's Inspector Morse operate, among other things, to 'brand-name' the fictions in which they appear; but it would seem odd to take the first Marples/Campion/Morse novels as originals to which subsequent novels are sequels.

2. Joel E. Siegel's *Val Lewton: The Reality of Terror* (London: Secker and Warburg, 1972), on which I shall be relying heavily in what follows, provides an exemplarily detailed account of why 'auteurising' Lewton is justified. A key factor here is Lewton's uncredited script input: 'I am and have always been a writer–producer,' Lewton writes (to his mother and sister!), in a letter in which he laughingly corrects 'your ignorance of the "moom picture industry" as she industrates' (Siegel, p. 23).

3. I am using the term 'prequel' here in a non-standard way. Normally, a prequel is itself a sequel, but one which diegetically goes back in time from the original film rather than forward (obvious example: *Butch and Sundance: The Early Days*). What I want to get from the term is a gestalt-shift effect whereby one could see *Cat People* as pre-*Curse* as much as seeing *Curse* as post-*Cat*. Of course, *The Curse of the Cat People* does 'come after' *Cat People* in fact, and the reversal of perspective is correspondingly artificial – but perhaps no less instructive for that.

4. Not surprisingly, since he was George Sanders's brother.

5. Siegel, p. 135.

6. Amy posts invitations to her birthday party in a hollow tree, because she believed her father when he said it was a magic postbox. She actually has quite a good birthday party without guests (the 'gentleness' of the film, as always, is striking), but the schoolmates who had been told they were to be invited and then weren't are understandably somewhat cross.

7. This is the plot as foreseen, and as publicised, by the studio, after all. Siegel is amusing on this: 'As usual RKO decked out the film with moronic promotional tag-lines like "The Black Menace Creeps Again!" and "Sensational Return of the Killer-Cat Woman" ... Once again there were the bizarre suggestions for exhibitors. "Stencil paw prints leading to your theatre." "Send out a small group of men and women wearing cat masks to walk through the streets with cards on their backs reading 'Are cats people?' Schedule their routes so that they appear before the gates of defense factories when the various shifts are changing"' (p. 58). More surprisingly, this is the plot that the BFI's own SIFT information system assigns to the film in its one-sentence plot summary: 'The child of a second marriage is haunted for some time by the first wife who believed herself able to change into one of the cat tribe.'

8. Siegel, p. 137.

9. Siegel's final plot-summary version does bring out Irena's 'presence' in the scene, but treats it as simply imaginary: 'just before Oliver arrives with the police, Barbara is calmed when Amy, summoning Irena to her aid and confusing her with Barbara, calls her "my friend"' (p. 140). Siegel was writing long before video, and I certainly don't want to score points on accuracy against him, but the complexity of the sequence is witnessed to by the real difficulty it poses to the paraphrase enterprise;

94

the superimposition of Irena upon Barbara just *has more weight* than the phrase 'confusing her with' acknowledges.

10. The detailing of the final sequence is again subtle. Oliver holds the almost-asleep Amy in his arms outdoors, looking out over the garden. 'Amy, from now on you and I are going to be friends. [The last time this word will be spoken in a film which so obsessively returns to it.] I'm going to trust you. I'm going to believe in you. You'll like that, won't you?' Amy responds affirmatively but wearily (there is no reason to believe that here any more than elsewhere in the two films Oliver is being let off the hook of 'the pedestrian' by Lewton). Oliver then looks up from the child in his arms and outwards, after which he says, 'Is your friend in the garden? Can you see Irena now?' Amy cautiously looks up. Shot of Irena in the garden, smiling. Amy, now much more animatedly and happily, says, 'Yes, I can see her.' Oliver: 'I can see her too, darling.' Oliver, however, is not at this point looking into the garden, but into Amy's eyes. Both register great happiness in their 'pact', and Oliver carries Amy into the house. The final shot is of the snowy garden with Irena standing there and then disappearing, leaving the screen uninhabited for a few seconds before the music rises for a typical RKO 'The End'. The crucial question, of course, is what 'I can see her too, darling' means. What *doesn't* happen is that Oliver looks up and out at the image of Irena we have been shown. He just might have seen Irena in his survey of the garden *before* asking, 'Can you see Irena now?' However, it seems more likely that he has not literally seen Irena; but in saying he has, is he lying, or is he expressing a sort of new empathy with Amy which would make the expression something much more complicated than a lie? The film's whole reparative thrust must be towards the latter possibility, though the former (the 'harder) reading is not excluded by what we see. And how are things affected by the fact that we, the audience, 'see her too', and see her fade, too?

11. It should be acknowledged that the film's exclusion of Amy's real mother Alice from its final sequences is probably its most hard-to-defend feature.

12. A taste of such a reordering is given in one of the most striking essays of the 1980s, J. F. Lyotard's 'Domus and the Megalopolis' (in *The Inhuman*, Cambridge: Polity Press, 1991, pp. 191–204). Lyotard evokes, against the universalising and uncontestable systems-rationalism of 'Development' today, a sort of ideal-type of the bucolic, Mediterranean style, itself drawn in broad enough strokes to have a certain kitsch effect; then he dramatises – and still, and perhaps as even more effectively *against*, Development – a grim transform of that bucolic: 'In this scene, the female servant with the heart of gold is impure. The service is suspect, ironic. The common work is haunted by disaster. . . . The domestic monad is torn, full of stories and scenes, haunted by secrets. Acts of violence stretch it to breaking point, inexplicable injustices, refused offers of affection, lies, seducations accepted and unbearable, petty thefts, lusts. Freud makes us reread, via Sophocles and Shakespeare, the tragedy of the Greek families in this penumbra of madness. . . . Father, mother, child, female servant with the heart of gold, niece, old man servant, shepherd and ploughman, gardener, cook, all the figures of wisdom, the corner of the park under the fig tree, the little passages for whispering, the attic and

its chests – everything is matter for obscene crimes. Something in the *domus* did not want the bucolic' (pp. 195–6). Irena, Dr Judd, and the whole cat-people mythos in *Cat People* might be characterised in terms of this 'haunted' scene, as against the (anxious) bucolic of Oliver and Alice.

13. Siegel, p. 27 (quoting DeWitt Bodeen); cf. p. 41: 'Even before shooting commenced on *Cat People*, Koerner told Lewton that his second project would be based on an article called "I Walked With a Zombie" by columnist Inez Wallace, which had appeared in the *American Weekly* magazine. Mark Robson remembers that Lewton's face was white and his manner impossibly gloomy when he returned from that meeting with Koerner. . . . His associate dreaded his arrival the next morning, but Lewton came in unusually early and in an inexplicably gay mood. He called his staff together and announced that in the guise of a zombie chiller, he would make a West Indian version of *Jane Eyre*.'

14. Siegel, p. 57. Note how the alternative title involves a doubling pun: Amy and her *amie*. The speculatively inclined may enjoy thinking of this against (i) Lewton's mother's first name, Nina; (ii) the doubling name of the actress playing 'friend', Simone Simon.

15. Siegel, p. 28, quoting a Lewton diary entry.

16. Siegel, p. 28.

17. Siegel, p. 7.

18. Siegel, p. 7.

19. Siegel. pp. 7–8. In terms of the *name* question, would it be fanciful to juxtapose with these family facts and later facts to do with the Lewton films' names, so disguised or problematic, as per the RKO management's game? (Verna De Mots (!), Lewton's secretary: 'Charles Koerner kept dreaming up those outrageous titles to stick him with' (Siegel, p. 40); Ruth Lewton: 'As Mrs Lewton says: "I would never go to see a movie called *I Walked With a Zombie* unless somebody dragged me there"' (Siegel, p. 44).) Did anything in Lewton *will* such a naming game?

20. Siegel, p. 8.

21. Siegel, pp. 11–12.

22. Siegel, pp. 14–15.

23. Siegel, p. 13.

24. Siegel, p. 24.

25. Siegel. p. 7.

26. Siegel, p. 59.

27. Siegel, p. 33. Compare Conway's brother, George Sanders, born in 1906: 'My parents were not members of the nobility nor were they terribly rich. But as most people seemed to be in those days, they were well-off. They were both born in St Petersburg but were not orthodox Russians, since their ancestors came from Scotland. My mother was descended through her grandmother from the Thomas Clayhills of Dundee, who went to Estonia in 1626 to establish a business there. . . . [In 1917] the Tsar and his family were shot, along with most of our relatives and friends.' (*Memoirs of a Professional Cad*, London: Hamish Hamilton, 1960, pp. 12, 18.)

28. Visually, the effect of the redemptive superimposition of Irena over Barbara is not without its own eerie sense of prequelling the anti-redemptive

superimposition of the skull of 'Mother' over Norman's head at the end of *Psycho*. The relationship of Hitchcock to Lewton would be worth exploring. Amy's frightened examination of Julia's sitting-room (the 'old woman space') is visually echoed by Vera Miles's exploration of 'Mother's' bedroom. More crucially, the theme of grown daughter seemingly unloved by mother, who indeed showers affection on a little girl who is not a blood relation, becomes, of course, the central dynamic of *Marnie*. This is where Hitchcock chooses to 'be redemptive': he contrives a reparative version of Barbara–Julia–Amy *sans* Irena and with maximal investment in 'Barbara'.

BUT WHAT IF BEAUTY IS A BEAST?

Doubles, Transformations and Fairy Tale Motifs in *Batman Returns*

Duncan Petrie

In this essay I want to demonstrate the contemporary resonance of aspects of classical fairy tale in mainstream cinema by way of an analysis of Tim Burton's film *Batman Returns*, one of the biggest box office hits of 1992 in both the UK and North America. My focus here will be specifically on the question of adult-centred (as opposed to child-centred) fantasy because, despite its popularity with adolescents in their early teens, the narrative of *Batman Returns* is largely a meditation on questions of sexuality and fantasy. Furthermore, unlike several of the films discussed by Marina Warner in this volume, it features adult protagonists. One of the key motifs in this film, borrowed from fairy tale and folklore, is that of transformation. This usually involves a human being changing into some sort of animal, the best-known examples from the traditions noted above being the Werewolf and the Man/Beast from *Beauty and the Beast*. In *Batman Returns* (and its inferior predecessor, *Batman*, directed by Burton in 1989) transformation involves the adoption of a totemic animal, signified by the wearing of a costume and a mask, rather than a physical change as such. But the process of dressing up and wearing a mask goes beyond the realm of mere disguise. The issue of transformation in the Batman films is also profoundly influenced by aspects of nineteenth-century Romanticism, in particular the idea of the divided self or double.

As a film-maker, Tim Burton's *oeuvre* is heavily identified with comic-book/fairy tale subject-matter to which he tends to bring a suitably robust and fast-paced cinematic treatment. In addition to the two Batman films, his features to date include the pop art inspired *Pee-wee's Big Adventure* (1986), the comedy-horror *Beetlejuice* (1988) and *Edward Scissorhands* (1990), a reworking of the Frankenstein myth which combines aspects of a gothic and a pop art sensibility. Burton's approach to Batman has been to eschew the camp caped-crusader image of the popular 60s television series of my own childhood, which starred Adam West and Burt Ward as Batman and Robin, in favour of the darker, 'troubled' Batman of the original comic books created by artist Bob Kane and writer Bill Finger[1] and (particularly) recent reworkings such as Frank Miller's *The Dark Knight Returns* and *Batman: Year One* and Alan Moore's *The Killing Joke*.

Consequently, the first *Batman* film was deemed too violent and 'disturbing' for the usual 'PG' certificate and was the first to receive the new '12' rating category from the British Board of Film Classification. Similarly, *Batman Returns* was awarded a '12' certificate when it was released in Britain three years later. Indeed, *Batman Returns* in particular becomes really interesting at precisely those moments where it begins to strain on its BBFC rating: that is, in its representations of eroticism and violence.[2] However, as a substantial amount of money was spent on the production and marketing of *Batman* and *Batman Returns*, the economic imperative in each case was to reach a mass audience, including the highly significant teenage market. The compromises which such considerations impose on film-makers are exacerbated in the case of the Batman phenomena as these cinematic texts are located within a web of multimedia commercial interests controlled by US corporate conglomerate Time–Warner.[3]

The production of the two Batman films should also be seen in a context of the increasing influence of comic books on the choice of subject-matter in Hollywood and, more crucially, on the aesthetics of visual style and narrative construction. In addition to Burton's work, examples of the kind of film I am alluding to include the *Superman* trilogy, *Who Framed Roger Rabbit?*, *Dick Tracy* and the *Teenage Mutant Ninja Turtle* films. Stylistically, this kind of film has come to rely more and more on the creation in the studio of a kind of cinematic analogue of the world of comic books, with characters and plot structure to match. In *Roger Rabbit* the mix of live action and animation illustrates in graphic terms the kind of developments I am alluding to, while *Dick Tracy* boasts sumptuous sets and almost pop art visuals, the pages of a comic book (almost literally) brought to life.

In a similar vein, the cinematic staging of the action in the Batman films helps to reinforce a reading in which the realm of the comic book dovetails with that of classical fairy tale. Anton Furst's original conception of Gotham, reworked by Bo Welch in the sequel, is a nightmarish vision of an urban dystopia. Peter Wollen notes that the design of the city in *Batman Returns* is modelled on Hugh Ferris's 1920s 'vistas of an imaginary Manhattan and Harvey Wiley Corbett's schemes for a city of multilevel arcades joined by bridges spanning the void between urban cliffs'.[4] For Wollen, Gotham is a perfect example of the imaginary city as a 'psychic projection rather than a sociological delineation'. The creation of a fantasy environment in which the cinematic action is staged and contained helps to define the two Batman films as fairy tale fantasies, occurring in a dream-scape.

Although my primary focus here is on *Batman Returns*, it is necessary to sketch in some of the background to the character of Batman provided by the earlier film. It introduced the Batman as an ambiguous presence, the citizens of Gotham initially unable to discern whether this shabby figure is a force for good or evil, vigilante or vampire. As Kim Newman observes, his 'costume – all black rather than shades of blue and gray – is rather more reminiscent of Dracula or the Phantom of the Opera than of Batman's red-white-and-blue-hued super-heroic competitors Superman and Captain America'.[5] Consequently, for most of the film the 'official' forces of law and order are unsure of whether to treat Batman as friend or foe.

The true identity of Batman, millionaire businessman Bruce Wayne, is revealed early on in the narrative. Wayne is a self-obsessed, brooding loner, living alone, save for his English butler Alfred, in the vast forbidding spaces of Wayne Mansion. This recalls the set of cavernous Great Hall of Xanadu (complete with huge fireplace) in *Citizen Kane* – indeed, Wayne's melancholic isolation echoes that of the elderly, increasingly tyrannical, Charles Foster Kane. His inability to give of himself, and thereby to participate in intimate relationships, is demonstrated by the rather clumsy manner in which he treats Vicki Vale: they sit at opposite ends of a vast banqueting table in a parody of what is supposed to be a cosy supper for two, compounded by the rather callous way he brushes her off after the two have slept together. However, it is through Vale's subsequent obsession to find out all she can about the enigmatic Wayne that we discover the reasons behind his tormented state of mind. His psychological state is the direct result of a childhood trauma caused by the experience of witnessing his parents being gunned down in cold blood by muggers. Since that moment Wayne had trained his mind and body for the time when he would inherit the family fortune, providing him with the material resources to dedicate his very existence to fighting crime, to purging the faceless evil in society which had destroyed his parents.

This vocation inevitably brings him into conflict with villain Jack Napier, a ruthless and extremely vain hoodlum who has fallen from favour of Gotham's crime boss Carl Grissom because he is dating Grissom's girlfriend behind his back. Grissom sets up Jack to be killed by the police (members of whom are on his payroll) during a raid on the Axis chemical works. Bruce Wayne gets wind of the plot and arrives on the scene as Batman. In the ensuing mêlée, Batman and Napier confront each other. Napier fires on his opponent who deflects the bullet which then ricochets and hits Napier in the face, knocking him over a parapet. Batman grabs him but Napier slips from his grasp into a large vat of bubbling toxic waste.

Miraculously he survives, but is a changed being. As a result of his immersion in the chemicals, plus the damage already done to his face by the bullet, his hair has turned green, his skin white, his face frozen into a demonic grin (the nerve endings apparently having been destroyed). This is all too much for the narcissistic Jack and his (already established) tendency towards crazed malevolence becomes magnified exponentially in his new persona of the Joker. In effect, he becomes the very antithesis of Batman who had (inadvertently) created him. As Uricchio and Pearson put it:

> Just as the Batman responded to his tragedy by dedicating himself to justice, the Joker responded to his by dedicating himself to perverse, absurdist crime. Both singlemindedly pursue their goals, the Batman striving to impose order on an unjust universe and the Joker doing his best to enhance the chaos of a meaningless world.[6]

It is later revealed that the young Jack Napier was the actual hoodlum who gunned down Bruce Wayne's parents – disclosed when he later asks Wayne, 'Did you ever dance with the devil in the pale moonlight? I always ask that of my victims,' the very words the murderer had uttered to the petrified Wayne as a child. This serves to complete the circle and bind the two characters together in a symbiotic relationship.[7]

Unfortunately, the relationship between the two doesn't quite work in the film, primarily because of an imbalance in terms of the two performances. Jack Nicholson as the Joker is the star of the film and the major selling-point in its marketing. He was also rumoured to have been paid $11 million to play the Joker – a significant portion of a budget variously reported as being somewhere between $30 and $50 million. The problem is, Nicholson knows he is the star and vigorously over-acts throughout as if to prove it. (This became something of a Nicholson trademark in the 80s.) Michael Keaton, on the other hand, actively downplays his role. He was not a popular choice with the fans, being seen as too lightweight a choice for the role of Batman with consequently little screen 'presence': indeed, Warners reportedly received 50,000 letters protesting at this casting decision. Whatever one's opinion of Keaton in the final analysis, the film is heavily unbalanced with the overwrought Nicholson totally dominating the proceedings.

But if the relationship between Batman and the Joker is interesting as a kind of doubling, then the character of Bruce Wayne is a particularly salient version of the split psyche or divided self. This theme is

doubling

101

central to much romantic literature and is identifiable in the work of James Hogg, Hoffman, Dostoyevsky, Maupassant, Robert Louis Stevenson and Edgar Allen Poe among many others.[8] Indeed, the notion of the fundamental duality of the human mind was a prevalent idea in the 19th century in both art and science, the physiological explanation resting on the idea that the two hemispheres of the brain were capable of separate and conflicting volitions. This intellectual consensus in turn helped to fertilise the soil from which the highly influential discipline of psychoanalysis would spring in the early 20th century. As Lionel Trilling has observed,[9] Freud's model of the unconscious relies heavily on the idea of the divided self which so obsessed many nineteenth-century Romantics.

The figure of the double has also been a popular motif in the cinema from the medium's formative years. Indeed, it is a film version of *The Student of Prague* (most likely the 1913 version directed by Stellan Rye) which the psychoanalyst Otto Rank takes as his starting-point in his seminal essay on 'The Double'.[10]

As Lucy Fischer points out, the double takes on diverse forms in literature and cinema, being either an ethereal being, such as a shadow, a reflection or a portrait, or an identical being, a person of kindred appearance or a twin.[11] However, in the case of *Batman* and *Batman Returns*, what we have is a third form: a split persona which does not involve an objective division of self and double (be it either an ethereal or an identical being) but is rather a subjective split where the individual undergoes some kind of psychic transformation, which may or may not involve some outward change in appearance ranging from the donning of a costume to actual physical change into some human or animal. The latter kind of transformation has been a popular motif in the horror film (particularly in werewolf films and the many cinematic adaptations of Stevenson's *Dr Jekyll and Mr Hyde*) because it can be rendered effectively in visual terms, utilising the magical possibilities of cinema.

So the persona of Batman is more than a mere mask which Bruce Wayne dons to conceal his true identity: Batman is a fundamental part of Wayne's fractured psyche, arising out of his childhood trauma. This *alter ego* is a shadowy vigilante who stalks the city at night with an air of melancholy resignation, recalling Bram Stoker's Count Dracula who laments at one stage, 'To die, to be really dead, that must be glorious.' The pathos is derived from a sense that Wayne is fulfilling a destiny over which he has little ultimate control. Furthermore, such a characterisation is demonstrably rooted in the literary tradition of the double alluded to above. As Karl Miller notes:

To discuss the literature of the Double is to discuss the literature of Solitude – what may be called the annals of the orphan or singleton. . . . Where the double is, the orphan is never far away, with secrecy and terror over all. To bring together the orphan and the double is to unite submission and aggression, freedom and impediment. Theirs is a proximity which is sometimes an identity.[12]

Bruce Wayne is himself an orphan, and the act of violence which rendered him thus also served to fracture his psyche. He is an outsider who frequently prefers to shut himself away in Wayne Mansion, and who is a lone crime-fighter. Interestingly enough, neither film includes Batman's familiar sidekick, Robin. This was a wise decision, given the general serious approach to the character which may have been undermined by the homoerotic undertones of the relationship between Batman and Robin in the television series, but also because of this necessity to have Batman a solitary figure. His duality is both an impediment (to forming proper fulfilling human relationships) and a freedom (to fight crime). His inability to act in the former sense (submission) is the flip side of his very ability to act in the latter (aggression).

Miller goes on to suggest that what he refers to as 'the literary tradition of Gothic strangeness' (the designs of the Batman films also owe much to the Gothic heritage) has been a refuge to the figure of the orphan, a typical device in such works being to find 'prospects and heritages for the forlorn'. It is Bruce Wayne's inheritance which makes Batman materially and technologically possible. The romantic tradition alluded to above grew out of the Gothic. In addition to orphans and doubles, a key motif of this literature identified by Miller is secrecy, which is a further crucial factor in the maintenance of the identity of Batman. Apart from Alfred, the only character permitted to 'know' the true identity of Batman in the first film is Vicki Vale. This is actually at the behest of faithful Alfred who believes Vicki to be therapeutic, a way of drawing Bruce Wayne out of himself.

This whole question of the divided self is compounded in *Batman Returns* by way of the character of Selina Kyle/Catwoman.[13] Miller notes that in 'the literature of duality . . . comparatively few women are awarded doubles, or write about them.'[14] However, Fischer argues that it is in the realm of cinema that we find the most interesting group of texts dealing with the female double. She also suggests that critical analyses of the double in literature has frequently related the double – 'a symbolic discourse expressing psychic conflicts' – to the schizoid or pathological consciousness of individual authors. Indeed, Rank explicitly explores the 'damaged' personalities of writers like Hoffman, Maupassant and Poe and attempts to relate this subjective dimension to their literary concerns. Fischer argues that by virtue of it being a collectively produced medium for a mass market, cinema is tied less to the subjectivity of the individual author and therefore resists scanning for traces of a unique psyche. On the other hand, and for the same reasons, it is a particularly fruitful medium for revealing the play of wider social forces and attitudes.[15]

The on-screen creation of the Catwoman is stranger and more visually powerful than anything in the first film. Selina Kyle is introduced as a wimpish, bumbling secretary, lacking in confidence and self-assurance and dressed in a rather frumpish brown twin set. She lives a lonely existence in her tacky apartment, decorated in pink, full of girlish knick-knacks such as cuddly toys and a doll's house. She obviously doesn't lack ambition, having become secretary to Max Schreck, one of the most powerful men in Gotham City. But she obviously wants a man to share her life – her instinctive response on entering her apartment is to call out, 'Honey, I'm home. Oh, I forgot, I'm not married.' Her cat, Miss Kitty, comes in through the window, hungry to be fed and Selina remarks, with more than a hint of envy, on her sexual exploits which are obviously more frequent than those of her owner. Selina listens to the messages on her answering machine, which include her mother berating her for leaving home to be a lonely secretary in Gotham, a sales call for Lady Gotham perfume, and an unidentified male cancelling a vacation. In other words, she is very much like the archetypal fairy tale princess waiting for her prince to come and carry her off on a white charger.

Yet right from the start we are not altogether comfortable with this portrayal of Selina Kyle. She is played by Michelle Pfieffer, one of Hollywood's top actresses, associated (particularly in the wake of films like *The Fabulous Baker Boys*) with sophisticated, 'sexy' roles. Despite the visual coding with the glasses, the physical clumsiness and the fluffy apartment, Pfeiffer's star persona works against our belief in this version of Selina and we await some kind of transformation to occur. We do not have to wait long.

She inadvertently uncovers a plot by Schreck to swindle the city by building a power plant which rather than generating electricity will actually drain power, and is caught in the act by her malevolent boss. After terrorising her, he pushes her out of the window which is several floors up and leaves her for dead in the wintry street below. In line with the traditional misogynist reactions as outlined by Marina Warner, Selina is punished for her curiosity. (Bluebeard)

Suddenly a cat (apparently Miss Kitty) appears and starts to lick her face, followed by several others who gnaw, scratch and lick her, presumably to bring her back from the edge of death. Eventually her eyes flicker open and she wanders home in a somnambulant daze. She drinks some milk normally reserved for Miss Kitty (the white liquid

104

running sensuously down her face) and listens again to her answering machine: more calls from mother and a follow-up sales pitch for perfume which suggests that its effect will be a late-night rendezvous in the office with the boss. This throws her into a fury and she proceeds to smash up her apartment, stuff her soft toys into the waste disposal, and spray-paint her clothes and doll's house. The neon sign which read 'Hello There' (a homecoming touch substituting a greeting from the absent partner) is altered to 'Hell here'. One item of clothing she does not destroy is a black leather or PVC raincoat which she sets about reconstructing into a new kind of attire: a sexy, fetishistic catsuit complete with nails. The transformation is completed when she appears fully clad at the window, the surrounding rooftops covered with cats – evoking *The Company of Wolves* (a film not dissimilar in theme) stretches sensuously and remarks, 'I don't know about you, Miss Kitty, but I definitely feel much more yummy.'

The meaning of this transformation is obviously the awakening of Selina's sexuality. Like Cinderella, Little Red Riding Hood and a host of fairy tale heroines before her, she learns to put away childish toys and become a woman. The coding of female sexuality through the feline register is a familiar device. As Prawer points out, while the male vampire is linked to the bat and the wolf, the figure of the female 'vamp' is associated with the serpent and the cat: 'Cat-women, leopard-women, and such abound in American movies, from *Tiger Woman* in 1917, to the *Island of Lost Souls* in 1932 or *Cat People* in 1942.'[16] What is interesting is that, while in all cases the beast is dangerous, in the classic examples from fairy tale it is also terrifying and horrific: Beauty has to learn to love the Beast. In the case of Selina Kyle/Catwoman the beast is extremely attractive, oozing a lethal mix of untamed sexuality and raw power.

While the feline often embraces rather misogynistic elements of female sexuality as cunning and dangerous (and this is not entirely absent from *Batman Returns*) to be feline is also to be self-reliant, which is something Selina as Catwoman never fully relinquishes. Indeed, the initial effect on the character of Selina is one of empowerment. She has freedom of movement: when we next see her it is prowling the night-time streets as a cat does (but also significantly as Batman does). Her physical awkwardness has been replaced by an athletic grace, she tumbles into action in the manner of a top gymnast. Out of costume she is also an infinitely more formidable character. The birth of Catwoman has entailed the death of the old Selina. When she turns up at work (much to the bafflement of Max Schreck) she is confidence and power personified. Her sensuality wins over Bruce Wayne (who is having a meeting with Schreck) in an instant and, totally out of character, he eagerly asks her for a date.

Like Batman, Catwoman is a vigilante but her motives are initially less clear. She attacks a would-be rapist with the immortal line, 'Be gentle, it's my first time,' before kicking him around and horrifically scratching his face (a similar effect is generated when Batman turns his Batmobile around and incinerates one of Penguin's henchmen), but then seems to have little sympathy for his intended victim, berating her for making it so easy for a Batman to come along to save her. She clearly believes, à la Camille Paglia, that women have to take more responsibility to achieve greater independence and power. While the relationship between Selina and Bruce Wayne is developing, the characters' alter egos are battling it out on the rooftops of Gotham City. Batman clearly perceives Catwoman as a threat and attempts to subdue her, which results in two violent encounters. In the first, Batman (mirroring Schreck, and then later Penguin) pushes Catwoman off a building. But like the mythical cat she has nine lives and it is not easy to get rid of her.

During their second rooftop altercation, Catwoman sits astride a stunned Batman and licks his face from chin to nose. This action, and the combination of Selina's S/M leather catsuit (the theme augmented by her use of a whip, symbolic of an 'absent' tail) and rubber batsuit costumes, generates a fetishistic encounter which is genuinely and powerfully erotic. The scene has two previous visual echoes in the film: the encounter between Bruce and Selina on the couch in Wayne Mansion where Selina lunges at Bruce in a moment of uncontrolled sexual passion, made rather problematic by the fact that both desperately try to hide wounds inflicted during their first violent encounter as Batman and Catwoman, and also the 'kiss of life' from Miss Kitty at the beginning of Selina's transformation.

Bruce and Selina are linked together in their common schizoid personas. Indeed, Selina's role as a 'woman on the verge' is a recasting of the chaos represented by the Joker which posits the antithesis of Bruce Wayne/Batman's obsession with control. In pop Freudian terms, therefore, Batman represents an overinvestment in the superego, while Catwoman can be seen as a representation of the dominant id. In fact, their union suggests a possible reconciliation of their two fractured personalities. Unfortunately, this is never allowed to happen. Paradoxically, unlike the earlier Bruce Wayne/Vicki Vale situation, their relationship is destined never to be consummated. The closest they get is in the scene at the masked ball (they are the only two who have turned up without masks because in a sense we know that they are already masks) when each realises who the other is after a chance remark about mistletoe which had been made during their second (erotic) rooftop encounter when the two were fighting. Batman remarked, 'Did you know mistletoe is poisonous if you eat it?' to which Catwoman replies, 'Don't you know a kiss is deadly if you mean it?' The deadly kiss comes when she fulfils her revenge on Schreck by taking a power line and a stun gun (which she kept as a memento from the first time she met Batman when he saved her from one of Penguin's henchmen before her transformation), and electrocuting her 'murderer' in a kiss of death. Before fulfilling her destiny she rejects the imploring Batman (who has revealed himself as Bruce Wayne) with the line, 'I'd love to be your princess and come and live with you in your castle. I just couldn't live with myself.' Wherein she brings the house down on Schreck and herself. Her independence is not to be compromised by visions of traditional romantic bliss.

What you effectively have in *Batman Returns*, therefore, is a rendering of the classic fairy tale romance which not only restores ambiguity to the characterisations, but rejects the neat resolutions of the traditional happy ending. The princess learns to put away her childish things and to become a woman, but she is ultimately unable to claim her prince: in fact, as I note above, she actively rejects him.

The character of the Penguin can also be appropriated into this schema. The film opens with the birth of the freak baby, later identified as Oswald Cobblepot, who has claws instead of hands. He is rejected by his parents who throw his crib into a river and watch it drift away into the sewers in a bizarre mix of the story of Moses with shades of *The Phantom of the Opera*. Like its predecessor, *Batman Returns* is replete with filmic references. The opening sequence outside Cobblepot Mansion, for example, is a take-off of the beginning of *Citizen Kane*, and Cobblepot's parents are clearly modelled on Cruella de Ville and her husband from Disney's *101 Dalmations*, the metaphor being the heartlessness of parents who would reject their role and abandon their helpless child. Thirty-three years later (another biblical allusion), we discover that the child has been raised by penguins and has become an extremely dangerous psychopath (a wonderful slobbering performance by Danny De Vito), hell-bent on revenge on the citizens of Gotham with his gang of circus performers (it transpires that he spent some of his childhood as a sideshow freak in a travelling circus).

Within the fairy tale reading of the film, the Penguin assumes the role of the wicked witch. Indeed, De Vito's make-up codes him as a witch with his pointed nose, his sharp teeth, rasping voice (reminiscent of Margaret Hamilton as the Wicked Witch of the West in *The Wizard of Oz*), the top hat which resembles a witches' hat, the umbrella which enables him to fly (the corollary of the broomstick) and his overall hag-like appearance. He commands his army of clowns in much the same way as the Witch in *The Wizard of Oz* commands her simian-like soldiers. But unlike all the archetypes in fairy tale this witch is a man.

However, in line with mysogynistic representations of the hag, as Marina Warner has demonstrated, the Penguin has, in spite of his gross, slobbering appearance, a bawdy sexual appetite. Unlike the Joker whose perverse pleasure lay in maiming beautiful women, the licentious Penguin fancies himself as a bit of a Lothario. He flirts outrageously with a totally uninterested Catwoman at one stage when the two join forces to remove Batman as an obstacle by framing him for kidnapping the Ice Princess and paving the way for Penguin to become mayor of Gotham and Catwoman to take her revenge outside the law. Penguin proposes a partnership along the lines of 'Beauty and the Beast' but she rejects him, disgusted by his lewdness, his blatant sexism and brutality (he kills the Ice Princess). This self-image as a sexual being renders the Penguin ridiculous and rather pathetic. He also, again in line with Warner's arguments, has a filthy tongue. Indeed, his first utterances of sexual inuendo directed at a female employee of Schreck are not only outrageous but deeply disturbing in their underlying ferocity. In this way the character of Penguin transforms the traditional misogynist representation of the old hag into the prime perpetrator of overt misogyny in the film.

So ultimately the unholy trio of 'The Cat, the Bat and the Penguin', as the publicity for the film put it, can be read as cyphers for the more familiar fairy tale line-up of Princess, Prince and Witch. In the first film Vicki Vale may have looked like a fairy tale princess in her white ballgown which she wears on her first visit to Wayne Mansion, but from the start she was always too 'knowing' to face the predicaments of the 'innocent' princess. She subsequently functions much more as a 'damsel in distress' who the Joker kidnaps and Batman has to rescue. In fact, he rescues her twice in the movie: the first time at the Museum when the Joker and his hoodlums set about destroying precious works of art, and then again at the final struggle in the bell-tower of Gotham Cathedral (a sequence which is straight out of *Vertigo*, Hitchcock's own masterpiece about fractured identity).

The three principal characters in *Batman Returns* have something else in common: the critical effect on them of absent parents. Both Bruce Wayne and Oswald Cobblepot are obsessed with the loss of their own parents (Penguin discovers the grave of the parents who abandoned him), and indeed, Wayne's own melancholic obsession provides him with a link to Penguin who he first sees on television pledging to find his parents. (Prompt for Alfred's remark, 'Perhaps you think there should be only one lonely man-beast in the city.') While Selina is not an orphan as such, she has left the security of the parental home and (symbolically) has not attained full adulthood status. In her own (pre-Catwoman) terms, she is in a transitory phase, between leaving her parents and finding a husband. If the pre-transformed Selina can be seen as a child, Max Schreck can be read as a metaphorical stepfather, the only significant adult authority figure present in her life and, like step-parents in fairy tales, malevolent and dangerous. Interestingly, Selina's subsequent existence as Catwoman is dedicated to revenging herself on Schreck (a different inflection of the revenge motive behind Batman – and, indeed, the Penguin).

In addition, the film is littered with references to parents and children, embracing the relationship between Schreck and Chip, the Penguin's plot to kill all the first-born sons of Gotham, his original publicity stunt – setting up the abduction of the Mayor's child and then apparently rescuing him, much to the adulation of the crowd, and Penguin's relationship with his army of penguins whom he affectionately refers to as 'my babies'.

To conclude, while I would argue that *Batman Returns* develops the fairy tale archetypes in interesting and sometimes progressive ways (the coding of the Witch as a man, the vulnerability of the Prince, and self-reliance, assurance and independence of the Princess), it still has its own problems which it is unable to resolve. The most apparent is the ultimately destructive force that is female sexuality. While Batman is sexually reticent, the Penguin grotesque, risible and ultimately pathetic, Catwoman's sexuality is positively dangerous. What is unleashed in Selina Kyle is too much for anyone (including her) to handle. Her sexuality cannot be contained and consequently (like the Penguin and the Joker) represents the ultimate threat to the rational order which Batman craves.

Of course, she also represents the ultimate in a male heterosexual masochistic fantasy: the lure of danger that is female. In fact, the manner in which she ultimately destroys Schreck is a graphic representation of the 'deadly kiss' on a par with an voluptuous vampire. In this sense, the representation of female sexuality in *Batman Returns* remains trapped in the realms of exotic (and deadly) otherness. While we may therefore have come some way from sanitised Victorian representations of the simpering, subjugated fairy tale Princess, moving back to the original 'earthiness' of the underlying thematics on the one hand and giving it a feminist inflection on the other, *Batman Returns* is ultimately unable to offer a real understanding of female sexuality and desire. Nevertheless, the fact that Michelle Pfeiffer ultimately steals the show, whether as object of desire or role model, shifts the issue to centre stage.

Notes

1. See Bill Boichel, 'Batman: Commodity as Myth', in Pearson and Uricchio (eds) *The Many Lives of the Batman* (London: BFI/Routledge, 1991).
2. I am flabbergasted that one British critic, Hugo Davenport writing in the *Daily Telegraph* (9 Feb. 1992), should come to the ingenious conclusion that, 'In many ways, *Batman Returns* is not a film for children at all.'
3. See Eileen Meehan, '"Holy Commodity Fetish, Batman!": The Political Economy of a Commercial Intertext', in Pearson and Uricchio, op. cit.
4. Peter Wollen, 'Delirious Projections', in *Sight and Sound*, August 1992.
5. *Monthly Film Bulletin*, September 1989.
6. Pearson and Uricchio, '"I'm Not Fooled By That Cheap Disguise"', in *The Many Lives of the Batman*, p. 198.
7. This relationship is the central theme of Alan Moore's graphic novel *The Killing Joke*.
8. See Karl Miller, *Doubles: Studies in Literary History* (Oxford University Press, 1985) and Otto Rank, *The Double: A Psychoanalytic Study* (Chapel Hill: University of North Carolina Press, 1971) for a discussion of this tradition in literature.
9. Lionel Trilling: 'Freud and Literature', in *The Liberal Imagination* (London: Mercury, 1961).
10. Rank, *The Double*.
11. Lucy Fischer, 'Sisters: The Divided Self' in *Shot/Counter Shot* (Princeton, NJ: Princeton University Press, 1989).
12. Miller, *Doubles*, pp. 22–39.
13. The original movie was a huge box office success (grossing $100 million in its first ten days in the USA and ending up the sixth highest grosser in history) and, following the logic of Hollywood, spawned the inevitable sequel. Despite having killed off the Joker in *Batman*, the film-makers were in the position of having several other characters, familiar from both the comic books and the television series, to draw upon. The obvious first choices were Batman's other two most famous criminal adversaries, Catwoman and the Penguin.
14. Miller, *Doubles*, p. 52.
15. Fischer, 'Sisters'.
16. S. S. Prawer, *Caligari's Children: The Film as Tale of Terror* (New York: Da Capo, 1980), p. 58.

COCTEAU FOR KIDS

Rediscovering *The Singing Ringing Tree*

Rosemary Creeser

Unlike the rest of the films included in the NFT's February 1992 season of *Fairy Tale and Film*, the East German fantasy film *The Singing Ringing Tree* had not been seen in British cinemas before its appearance late in autumn 1990 as part of the Junior London Film Festival. The reception the film received at this and subsequent screenings only serves to beg the question *why* a children's fantasy film made in the late 1950s by the state cinema of the former GDR, shot on a small-studio budget and using charming yet naive special effects, should have cast such a spell over British audiences.

By focusing on some of the main themes of the film this essay firstly seeks to unravel the separate constituents which have assigned it to the collective memory of those individuals who remember watching it when it was screened as part of the 60s children's television series *Tales from Europe*. A second but equally important objective is to outline the story surrounding its acquisition and subsequent distribution and to consider contemporary responses to the film.

A recurrent theme in fairy tales, and films like *The Singing Ringing Tree* which are based upon them, is that of transformation. In the film, although both the main characters undergo a physical transformation before they can live in true fairy tale fashion 'happily ever after', it is Princess Thousandbeauty's transformation which holds the strongest moral message, namely that physical beauty is not necessarily equated with goodness.

From the opening scene inside the fairy tale castle, when the princess rejects the prince's gift of a golden casket of pearls and demands that he brings her the seemingly impossible, a singing ringing tree, we are left in little doubt as to the princess's true character. Her expression of contempt as the pearls from the upturned casket pour down the steps and the rejected suitor leaves in search of the eponymous tree suggests that this is someone with an extremely elevated opinion of herself.

111

The Singing Ringing Tree (Francesco Stefani, 1988)

While superficially she has all the trappings of a beautiful fairy tale princess, complete with an elaborate 1950s Bardot-style coiffeur and a fairy tale crown (which, incidentally, she keeps on a silken cushion at her bedside) a succession of incidents only serve to confirm that this princess's beauty is 'skin deep', and that in fact she is haughty, vain and cruel. This cruelty manifests itself in her maltreatment of every living thing with which she comes into contact – not even the animals can escape. For example, in her haste to meet her father the king, who has returned with the singing ringing tree, she roughly pushes aside the palace dog who has come to greet his master. Then later, to make a place for the tree (that will neither sing nor ring), she orders her servant to empty the goldfish from the ornamental fountain in her garden.

The first of these incidents includes a common fairy tale motif – that of the returning father,[1] who, in exchange for his life, promises to relinquish the first thing that he meets on his return. In this case, in return for the magical tree that his daughter craves, the king gives his assurance, believing that he will first be met by his dog. Tragically, the princess's actions combine to bring about her fall from grace, her exile from the palace and subsequent transformation.

Only when she enters the Magic Kingdom and falls under a spell, causing her to lose her beauty, may the transformation commence. This requires that she put aside her misguided notions of superiority ('Me pick berries? I am a princess!') and help the bear and the other

112

fantastic creatures which inhabit the kingdom, and oppose the actions of the wicked dwarf.

By being kind she not only wins their affection but regains some part of her former beauty. However, it is the first of these which is most significant in terms of her transformation. Soon after her arrival in the Magic Kingdom the princess *demands* that the bear explain why all her attempts to befriend the animals have failed. Has he perhaps put a spell on them? In no uncertain terms, the cruel truth is revealed to her: unlike the humans who have previously been captivated by her beauty, animals only see her true nature. She is informed this is not irreversible, however, and that she can win their affections by being kind to them and learning to love someone other than herself.

In the subsequent scenes the dwarf uses his evil powers to wreak havoc on the inhabitants of the Magic Kingdom, firstly by creating a violent storm, then by turning the waterfall and the pool it feeds into ice by causing a freak snowstorm, and finally by destroying the Utopian shelter that the princess and the bear have built. Following each of these incidents the princess attempts to restore harmony by helping to rescue the animals affected by the dwarf's cruel actions, often at the risk of her own personal safety. In one scene we see her, barefoot, staggering precariously across the surface of the frozen pool to free the giant goldfish trapped in the ice, and then up to her neck in snow when she goes to rescue the golden-antlered horse that has got caught in a deep snowdrift.

After each of these events the princess regains some of her former beauty and is therefore closer to her final goal. Even when her transformation is seemingly complete and she has regained all of her coiffured bottle-blonde beauty the dwarf tries to trick her into leaving the Magic Kingdom – firstly by offering a luxuriant four-poster bed, a silver bath and golden plates (all of which she declines) and then by successfully deceiving her into believing that her father is dying. Without delay the princess returns to the palace only to discover that, quite to the contrary, her father is alive and well.

The final stage of the princess's transformation occurs when she has learnt to love someone other than herself (as signified by the words 'dear bear'). In the palace garden she eventually realises that she has been duped by the dwarf (who has misled her about the bear's true nature) and that the bear is in fact the spurned suitor who came to seek her hand in marriage, forced to assume the form of a bear. Finally, the once silent tree begins to sing and ring.

To complete the transformation process the princess must return once more to the Magic Kingdom, for the prince will only be free of his bearskin if the magic tree sings and rings there. In the penultimate scenes the dwarf tries his utmost to prevent her return, by placing an impenetrable thorn hedge in her path, then by destroying the stone bridge which is the sole route into the Magic Kingdom and by flooding the surrounding land. However, the fantastic creatures she has befriended come to her rescue. In a series of charming effects she is carried on horseback straight over the thorn hedge, across the water on the fish's back, and through the air on a floral swing suspended by a flock of white doves.

In spite of the dwarf's attempts she returns the tree to its rightful home. A tumescent flash of lightning illuminates the sky and simultaneously signals the demise of the malevolent dwarf, who disappears into the ground, Rumpelstiltskin-style. Finally, the prince assumes his former, human form and the happy couple prepare to return to the palace for a new life together.

In *The Singing Ringing Tree* the princess's beauty and subsequent transformation conveys the message that things are not always what they seem. In an examination of the role of beauty in fairy tale, Luthi[2] refers to this as 'the theme of appearance versus reality'. Conforming to the fairy tale form, which portrays an ordered world in which arrogant and haughty ways are incompatible with physical beauty, the princess in the film has to undergo a transformation causing her to temporarily trade her flawless complexion and bottle-blonde coiffeur for dark matted locks, a swarthy skin and a nose which cries out for reconstructive surgery. As well as conforming to contemporary sexual stereotypes of beauty, the initial portrayal of the princess as a blonde typifies a fairy tale fascination with golden objects. For example, Luthi notes that gold is used as an expression of the highest degree of beauty and that in the fairy tale genre beautiful characters frequently have golden hair, even in southern countries where this is much less common.

The princess's loss cruelly demonstrates the transience of beauty and shows that what is important in life is to be good and to reject worldly goods, for goodness will eventually overcome evil. Evil, in this case in the form of the wicked dwarf, is ever present. Throughout the film he always seems to appear when least expected, from under the ground or behind one of the giant conch shells which are strewn across the Magic Kingdom. The princess's loss also demonstrates a theme explored by Luthi, namely that good may be hidden in bad. In his work on the role of beauty in fairy tale he summarises the following as fitting ends for 'cruel beauties':

> they can be healed, whether simply because, after ninety-nine unsuccessful suitors, finally the right one comes along, or because the helper of the hero in an artful operation draws the snakes out of the body of the beautiful girl so that subsequently she is just as

good as she is beautiful, or because the traces of her connection with evil are flogged and washed away through a determined purification process.

Although their use of symbolism has meant that fairy tales have frequently been interpreted from a psychoanalytical perspective, it is also important to consider the socio-historical origins of the tales. This is particularly relevant since we now know they were often substantially reworked by their collectors. It has been noted that in reconstituting the tales on which the film *The Singing Ringing Tree* is based,[3] the brothers Grimm were intent on retaining themes such as the triumph of good over evil to validate their bourgeois notions of a 'better world'. Zipes[4] reveals that, in addition to the feelings of loss and fear of separation following their father's early death, the brothers suffered extreme financial hardship and a decline in social status. For example, at one point, in order to provide for the family, the older brother Jacob decided to discontinue his law studies and to take up a position nearer home. As a result of these experiences, the brothers developed their ideas of a 'better world' – characterised by family loyalty, goodness, justice, industry and diligence – which were subsequently translated into their stories.

For this same reason great emphasis is placed on family loyalty throughout the Grimms' tales. Although at the start of the film Princess Thousandbeauty demonstrates total disrespect by rejecting the most recent of the suitors her father has assembled, once her transformation is complete we are presented with a picture of family loyalty. On hearing that her father is dying, the princess shows her dedication by returning immediately to be at his side.

Though it is common in many of the Grimms' fairy tales for the main characters to be instrumental in bringing about their own transformation, collaboration plays an important part. In illustrating this, Zipes notes that 'The new realm to which the Grimm protagonist succeeds is only made possible through his or her ingenuity and the help of other small creatures or outcasts.' In this sense the princess's transformation in *The Singing Ringing Tree* conforms to Zipes's taxonomy. Although it is the princess alone who comes to realise that the wicked dwarf has tricked her and that the bear is not what he seems, the animals in the Magic Kingdom play an important part at each stage of her transformation. Moreover, at the end of the film, the animals come to her rescue, enabling her to overcome the seemingly insurmountable obstacles the dwarf places in her way. It is significant that this would not have been possible had she not earlier won their affection: like many of the Grimms' heroes and heroines, she possesses no unusual physical or magical powers.

In the film the prince's transformation must assume secondary importance. From the outset there is little evidence that the prince shares the negative characteristics exhibited by the haughty, spoilt princess. On the contrary, he shows great patience and dedication when she scornfully casts aside his gift of a casket of pearls and demands that he bring her the singing ringing tree. Courageously, he makes the long journey to the Magic Kingdom, where he attempts to procure the magic tree from its owner, the wicked dwarf, by offering him gold and jewels. By doing so he shows an overdependence on worldly goods and then a lack of common sense as he agrees to the dwarf's request – to surrender himself if the tree fails to sing before sunset. Not unexpectedly, the tree remains silent and the prince is forced to assume the form of a bear.

Although the prince's actions indicate that he is not a complete paragon, his faults are minor when compared with those of the petulant princess. For this reason he does not really *have* to change. In the film his transformation serves a different purpose – to awaken the princess to his positive characteristics and to teach her kindness. Throughout their stay in the Magic Kingdom there are subtle signs that the bear/prince is basically good. The animals do not shy from him in the way they do from the princess, and he is not too proud or arrogant to carry out ordinary tasks. Once the princess's transformation is complete and the magic tree has broken its silence he is quickly able to assume his earlier, human form.

The prince's metamorphosis into a bear is another typical fairy tale motif. For example, Von Franz[5] states that in fairy tales involving redemption (that is to say, those in which the main character or characters have been cursed or bewitched and have to undergo a series of events in order to be redeemed), protagonists are frequently required to assume the form of a number of animals, including that of the bear, wolf, lion and snake.

More recently, Warner[6] reveals that the bear has become the most popular manifestation of the Beast in the many versions of the fairy tale story of *Beauty and the Beast*, elements of which are found in *The Singing Ringing Tree*. Moreover, she identifies a growing preponderance in this century of less fearsome and altogether more sympathetic versions of the bear. The bear in *The Singing Ringing Tree* exemplifies this trend, which Warner attributes both to the fashion for teddy bears and to a growing concern with the wilderness and the creatures which inhabit it. Although it is hard to ascertain to what extent the co-writers of the film were influenced by the first of these, the influence of prevailing ideas regarding nature is clear. The way in which the bear is portrayed living in harmony with his surroundings reflects this. For example, in one scene we see the bear contentedly collecting berries from one of the bejewelled trees that punctuate the landscape, surrounded by a flock of white doves, several of which are perched on his shoulders.

Writers such as the psychoanalyst Bruno Bettelheim have found further meaning in the bear transformation motif. In *The Uses of Enchantment: The Meaning and Importance of Fairy Tales*, he considers those stories characterised by the motif of the 'animal groom', in which one partner (frequently, but not always, the male) undergoes a process of transformation, from a beast to a magnificent person. The message conveyed by these stories is that, for true love to prevail, there has to be a radical change in previously held attitudes about sex. According to his analysis of *Beauty and the Beast*,[7] Beauty learns to relinquish her Oedipal attachment to her father and to make another, equally fulfilling relationship with a member of the opposite sex (the Beast), with whom she discovers her own sexuality. In Stefani's film, by demanding that the prince first bring her a singing ringing tree, the princess is able to exert her free will and by so doing postpone the date when she will have to comply with her father's wishes for an arranged marriage. Significantly, to reach the magic tree at the end of the film the princess has to walk through a ring of flames, placed in her way by the wicked dwarf. On a purely symbolic level this may be interpreted as a symbol of her growing passion for the prince/bear and an acceptance of her sexuality.

In order for transformation to take place in *The Singing Ringing Tree* the prince and princess must enter another, magic world (the Magic Kingdom) separated from the human world (reality) by a stone bridge and a narrow tunnel. These are used to emphasise the characters' transition between worlds. In particular, the prince's entrance and first impression of the Magic Kingdom is accentuated by the use of evocative sound effects (reminiscent of a Hammond organ) and by the fact that he has to actually use his sword to slice through the dense cobwebs which line the tunnel walls. Once inside he enters a world so completely different from the one he has left that it bears no resemblance to it – a beautiful landscape punctuated by gigantic swathes of coral foliage, golden willow and bejewelled fruit trees, luminous kryptonite-like rocks and larger than life-size conch shells. To complete the picture, the Magic Kingdom is populated by strange, fantastic creatures which include a giant goldfish, a beautiful white horse with golden antlers and, of course, the wicked dwarf. The film's designers successfully evoke the illusion of another world with its own time and weather, similar to the magical world in which dreams are set. Inside this magic world the sun never sets and, with the exception of the storms created by the dwarf, no trace of weather appears to permeate.

Like many of the stories collected by the brothers Grimm, *The*

Singing Ringing Tree is infused with a powerful Utopian motif. In many ways the Magic Kingdom in the film conforms to ideas of a Utopian community based upon a symbiotic relationship between the gifts of nature (earth, water, air) and the potential of human co-operation. Inside the Magic Kingdom the princess's basic needs for food and shelter are provided for, as long as she puts aside her former ideas and is prepared to co-operate with the bear by helping him to build a shelter, to collect berries to eat and moss to sleep on. The first of these is important in the sense that it marks the onset of the princess's transformation. When the painstaking process of building the shelter is at last over ('One thousand bundles of stones and it will be complete') a flock of doves surround her as she decorates the cave entrance with a garland of flowers. As the camera clearly shows, she can hardly contain her joy since, until this point, all the creatures in the Magic Kingdom have shunned her. The Utopian theme is reiterated by the clever ways in which the main characters use the natural resources at their disposal. In one scene the bear uses a giant shell to help the princess free the golden-antlered horse that has got caught in a snowdrift, while in an other the princess uses one of the fantastic flower petals to gather berries.

As the responses in the later sections demonstrate, the inclusion of a magic, Utopian world is possibly one of the main factors that caused the film to have such a profound effect on those who first saw it in the 60s. Heinberg[8] reveals in a cross-disciplinary study of memories and visions of paradise that 'the vision of paradise fires the human imagination as few other ideas, images and dreams have ever done', and for this reason he suggests it is only natural that these images should evoke such a powerful response.

ACQUISITION OF THE FILM AND ITS SUBSEQUENT DISTRIBUTION

Several extremely enthusiastic conversations early in 1988 prompted my decision to bring *The Singing Ringing Tree* back into distribution. Although these conversations awakened vivid childhood memories of a magical, bejewelled garden inhabited by a princess, a dwarf and a pitiful bear, I was unable to remember what exactly had happened to the characters and who had ended up with *The Singing Ringing Tree*. What I was certain of, however, was that I had to find out what had happened to this marvellous film and if possible to bring it back into distribution for all those *aficionados* like myself who craved to see it again.

Early detective work in the BFI library uncovered a mysterious contact address in East Berlin. Perhaps not surprisingly, in the days leading up to the demise of the Berlin Wall, my attempts to establish contact with the rights holders of the film were far from simple. Much later I was to discover that I was not the first to beat steps to the East Germans' door. Several years earlier Louise Brierley, a children's book illustrator, had made a number of unsuccessful attempts to obtain information for an illustrated children's book inspired by her recollections of the film.[9] A sackful of unanswered letters later, I enrolled the help of the British Cultural Attaché in Berlin (for what are Cultural Attachés for but to effect cultural relations between countries?). Eventually, I received a reply from East Germany. Shortly after the fall of the Wall, I flew with trepidation to Berlin to see the film for the first time in twenty-four years.

I need not have worried. As soon as the house lights dimmed and the projector leapt into action in that dusty preview theatre on the banks of the Spree all the images that had lived at the back of my mind came flooding back. As I sat and watched the film again I soon realised that *The Singing Ringing Tree* was still a marvellous fantasy film and that I was right to want to bring it back into distribution. Turning to more practical issues, I also knew that, up against the competition from children's films distributed by major American distributors, a rediscovered children's film from Eastern Europe needed to be premièred in a very special venue.

Fortunately, I had early on enlisted the support of the programmer responsible for the children's section of the annual London Film Festival. Later in the year, when prints of the film finally arrived in the country, an enthusiastic selection committee broke with tradition (the festival normally only screens new films not previously screened in the UK) and selected the film for inclusion in the 1990 Junior London Film Festival.

Though I had always believed in the film, the queues at its first screening served as confirmation that there were many individuals like myself who wanted the opportunity to see it once more – and in many cases to introduce their own children to a film that had given them so much enjoyment. Like all good fairy tales, the story of the film's acquisition and subsequent distribution has a happy ending. *The Singing Ringing Tree* continues to be screened to audiences of adults and children in repertory cinemas around the UK, often as part of thematic programmes based around the themes of fairy tale and fantasy.

'WONDERFUL MEMORIES OF WHEN I WAS SEVEN'
(GUY, AGED 30)
Even before *The Singing Ringing Tree* had been brought back into distribution there was ample evidence that the film had rooted itself in the collective consciousness of those who remember seeing it first in the 60s. The film has been and continues to be a source of in-

spiration for contemporary film and video directors, artists and musicians. To my knowledge it has inspired an excellent illustrated book and a children's play, along with a few rather dubious 'indie' bands which have taken its name.

At many screenings of *The Singing Ringing Tree* the demographic characteristics of the audience alone suggest that the generation who first saw the film when it was serialised in the 60s by the BBC has never forgotten it. This section of the essay considers the responses of some of those who first remember seeing the film twenty or more years ago, who are now aged approximately between thirty and thirty-five. It attempts to summarise the elements of the film they remember, to assess the extent to which it has 'stood the test of time' and to describe in what way, if at all, it (or indeed they) have changed. The quotations that are used here and in the final section include responses to a questionnaire completed by those who saw the film at the NFT and transcripts of interviews given after a screening at the Phoenix Cinema in East Finchley, North London.

It is interesting to consider why images from *The Singing Ringing Tree* had such a profound and long-lasting effect on those who first remember seeing the film so many years ago. Without doubt the film includes some extremely strong visual images, particularly those involving some sort of incarceration (such as those where the fish gets trapped in the ice and the horse has got caught in a snowdrift), which, as the following quotes demonstrate, have had a lasting effect.

'I remember the horse, I remember the princess looking very ugly. I remember the fish getting stuck in the ice.'

'When I was a child in the 60s I saw what I now realise must have been the middle episode on TV. It ended with the fish stuck in the ice. All these years I've wondered what happened – it was really nice to find out.'

Not surprisingly, some of the most vivid recollections are of the princess, the bear and the (wicked) dwarf. The image of the dwarf, as reflected by the responses below, appears to have left a particularly strong and unpleasant impression on some of the children who first saw the film in the 60s – in some cases to such an extent that he *still* turns up in their dreams.

'I remember the dwarf and how scared I was.'

'. . . a very malevolent character . . . who leaps out at you from all sorts of nooks and crannies.'

'. . . a dwarf of such terrifying malevolence that he still turns up in my dreams.'

But let us also take into account the social context in which the film was first screened. Peggy Miller, the producer originally responsible for selecting the film for the BBC, has offered another explanation for its longevity, namely that during this time British children had experienced a starvation of this type of visual fantasy. Furthermore, in comparison with the West, the Eastern Europeans had a rich legacy of folklore, which they were particularly good at interpreting through film. She suggests that children in the mid 60s had quite literally never seen anything like *The Singing Ringing Tree* before, and for this reason it left a profound and lasting impression.[10]

While many of those who had seen the film so long ago had retained vivid visual images, these were often disjointed and incomplete. What were important, as the next quotation demonstrates, were the strong feelings (that had remained) of a strange, dream-like world in which they had no control, where they did not really understand what was going on and where there was an omnipresent sense of malevolence, characteristic of fairy tale.

'. . . bells and ice and a sort of emptiness and distress, lots of abstract stuff. I couldn't tell you what the story was, other than there was this sort of malevolence and this little scuttling creature.'

Among those questioned there was an overwhelming confirmation that the film had lived up to the memories they had cherished for over twenty years, with possibly one exception – they weren't quite as scared.

'I thought it was very charming. I was really taken aback. It was very romantic.'

'It lived up to my expectations. I didn't find it as frightening as the first time I saw it as part of *Tales From Europe*.'

'A joy to see it again – pure nostalgia for the 60s children in the audience!'

For the majority who were able to suspend their disbelief, even the less sophisticated effects (in several scenes the dwarf's safety harness is clearly visible as he leaps between rocks) and the choice of a studio set did not appear to seriously detract from their enjoyment. In fact, many mentioned that the use of a studio set with its naive hand-painted backdrops only added to the film, by creating the atmosphere of a strange, enclosed other world which has its own logic, its own time, its own weather – in short, the world within which fairy tales and dreams are set.

'I believe that it gave the film a kind of other-worldly, enclosed atmosphere which suited the fairy/folk genre.'

Some of the differences mentioned by those who saw the film the second time around concerned the use of colour and sound. While the film was made in Agfacolor it was first screened on children's TV in black and white, with the original dialogue turned down and narrated by a plummy BBC narrator.

Although some of those interviewed missed the old narration (the film has now been carefully and economically subtitled) it was felt that the addition of colour actually enhanced their enjoyment of the film by giving the impression that they had stepped into one of the colour plates of one of the very best illustrated *Grimms' Fairy Tales*. Finally, several of those interviewed, as illustrated by the following quote, referred to the new-found importance of the film's moral message.

'I got a totally different impression of it this time. . . . The moral story was what was important to me this time. I just wonder what happened to the fish. She left it to die in the moat.'

However, there was a feeling that in some the ways *The Singing Ringing Tree* was out of step with contemporary ideas. These mainly concerned the preoccupation of the film with the equation of beauty equals goodness and the characterisation of the wicked dwarf. Especially on the subject of the dwarf, many of the adults questioned whether a contemporary adaptation would have chosen to attribute such potently wicked characteristics to a person of restricted growth.

'I THINK THAT IT WAS A LOT LIKE A FAIRY TALE' (MARGUERITE, AGED 9)

But what do the children of the 90s think about *The Singing Ringing Tree*? This final section looks at the responses of some of the children who saw the film when it was shown again. An attempt is made to summarise the elements of the film they enjoyed and to assess to what extent it still appeals to children.

One of the themes of the film that the children appeared to enjoy most was that of transformation. Even if this did not have their parents' seal of approval, enjoyment of the scenes focusing on Princess Thousandbeauty's physical transformation was mentioned by children of both sexes.

'I liked when the princess got ugly and she changed every time she was nice to an animal.'

'I liked the scenes when she changed her face from beautiful to ugly and then back.'

Unlike the older members of the audience, and probably as a result of their differential experiences, few of the children were scared of the dwarf and some even mentioned liking him and the scenes he appeared in.

'I liked the dwarf.'

'[I liked] when the dwarf put all the snow on the water.'

'. . . when the dwarf tried to play tricks on the people so she [the princess] couldn't help the animals.'

One of the doubts expressed in connection with the film's continuing appeal to children concerns its production values. It is suggested that the naivety of *The Singing Ringing Tree* will be lost on a children's audience raised on a diet of state-of-the-art special effects, fast-action cartoons and *Ninja Turtle* movies. However, the following quotations seem to indicate that the unsophisticated special effects and clever use of a studio set did not appear to detract from the children's enjoyment of the film.

'I loved the way they did the scenery at the back . . . it was really brilliant.'

'The child behind me in the audience was very engrossed and particularly worried about the plight of the fish. I think that the less sophisticated special effects seemed to work and she was able to suspend her disbelief (as was I).'

'I liked it when the fish came.'

Since its rediscovery *The Singing Ringing Tree* has continued to captivate audiences of all ages, regardless of its minimal technological input and naive special effects. This only serves to emphasise that while technology can assist in creating a fantasy film, it is not absolutely essential. For example, in other areas of film-making associated with fantasy, such as animation, some of the best results are still achieved with nothing more sophisticated than the use of simple cutouts and a pen. As this essay has shown, what is important is the ability to create the illusion of another world, completely different from the world we inhabit, in which individuals are temporarily able to suspend their disbelief to allow the characters to work their magic.

Notes

1. See, for example, Marina Warner's article, 'Beauty and the Beasts', *Sight and Sound*, October 1992, vol. 2 no. 6.
2. M. Luthi, *The Fairy Tale as Art Form and Portrait of Man* (Bloomington: Indiana University Press, 1987).
3. Although *The Singing Ringing Tree* credits state that it is derived from some of the stories collected and published in the 19th century by the Brothers Grimm, a careful search of the *Grimms' Tales* fails to reveal any story of the same name or with a direct connection to the film's plot. It can only be assumed that, having chosen to adopt several of the common themes and motifs, the director Franco Stefani and his co-writer Anne Geelhaer created a title for the film by juxtaposing fragments of the names of the *Grimms' Tales* – for example, *The Juniper Tree* and *The Singing, Soaring Lark*.
4. J. Zipes, *The Brothers Grimm: From Enchanted Forests to the Modern World* (New York and London: Routledge, 1980).
5. M. Von Franz, *The Psychological Meaning of Redemption Motifs in Fairy Tales* (Toronto: Inner City Books, 1980).

6. Marina Warner, 'Beauty and the Beasts', *Sight and Sound*, October 1992, vol. 2 no. 6, p. 6.
7. See Bettelheim, *The Uses of Enchantment: The Meaning and Importance of Fairy Tales* (London: Penguin, 1976).
8. R. Heinberg, *Memories and Visions of Paradise: Exploring the Universal Myth of a Lost Golden Age* (Wellingborough: Aquarian Press, 1989).
9. See L. Brierley, *The Singing Ringing Tree* (London: Walker Books, 1988).
10. An examination of the children's programmes screened on BBC television in the three successive weeks in 1964 and 1966 in which *The Singing Ringing Tree* was screened supports this explanation. Although children were presented with some innovative puppetry and animation, including the inimitable *Tales of the Riverbank*, *The Magic Roundabout* (see Geoff Tibballs, *The Golden Age of Children's Television*, London: Titan Books, 1991) and a cartoon series from Hungary called *Peter's Adventures*, none of the contemporary children's programmes interpreted the themes of fantasy and magic in the same way.

Acknowledgments

I should like to thank all the individuals who helped to bring *The Singing Ringing Tree* back into distribution, in particular Terry Staples, co-ordinator of the Junior London Film Festival, for his enthusiasm and continuing support. I should also like to thank Nicola Reynolds and Nigel (for initial inspiration), Susanne Von Der Ende, 'the three Clares' (Claire Barratt, Clare Binns and Clare Ward), Studio Dm and, most importantly, the children of all ages who generously gave time after the Junior London Film Festival/NFT and Phoenix Cinema (East Finchley) screenings to answer questions on the film.

'DOING THEM GOOD'

Terry Staples

In the former Communist countries of Eastern Europe, from the 30s until the 80s, the full resources of the state were available for the production of films for children, and these projects were given a high priority. In the USA, on the other hand, such specialised production has always been seen as unprofitable and unnecessary. In the UK, uniquely, the children's film movement has never received a penny in direct subsidy from the state, but has instead been sustained for over fifty years on the basis of a marriage between private philanthropy and corporate commerce.

In this essay I seek to trace the early development of specialised children's cinema in Britain, in terms of both exhibition and production; to examine its relationship with its counterpart in the USSR; to consider the effects of its protective paternalism; and to ponder its residue. By way of illustrating and providing evidence for my arguments I shall draw upon a number of sources including contemporary writings and documentation, my own memories of cinemagoing as a child and those of correspondents and interviewees, and recent reviewings of some of the films discussed.

Specialised screenings were first mooted in the 20s, when children were allowed to see absolutely any film that was being shown in a cinema. The only restriction was that if a film had been awarded an 'A' certificate by the British Board of Film Censors, then a child (designated as anyone under the age of under 16) had to be accompanied, at least at the ticket office, by an adult. Not surprisingly, such a system was widely abused; indeed, 'getting in' to see a film that you were not supposed to see has been a badge of honour among children ever since the setting up of viewing restrictions.

A mixture of public-spiritedness, and an eye for commercial potential, caused Sidney Bernstein, owner of the Granada cinema chain, to think differently. As he later put it:

> There are films, just as there are books, which have no intrinsic demerit, but which are unsuitable for a child. It may be that they

125

present images which require a mature experience for their interpretation, or which, in the child's mind, are divorced from their context and acquire a wrong emphasis.[1]

At the same time, Bernstein was also concerned about the effect that children had on box office takings. He wanted to reduce children's presence at ordinary screenings on the grounds that 'at a grown-ups' performance children are a nuisance, whether fidgeting, expressing vehement enthusiasm, or clamorously displaying boredom', and that 'it is bad business if seats sold at half price could have been sold at full price'.

In March 1928 Bernstein tried to do something about it by initiating the first serious experiment of its kind in the UK – a planned series of Saturday morning performances of selected films at Granada cinemas in Willesden, Enfield, Leytonstone and Edmonton. (At Willesden, on the first day, so many children came that 200 had to be turned away.) Titles shown in these four cinemas included: *Peter Pan*, *Cinderella*, *Nelson*, *Rin Tin Tin*, *Robinson Crusoe*, *The Thief of Baghdad*, Chaplin's *The Circus*, *The Wonderland of Big Game*, *Dinner Time at the Zoo*, the *Felix the Cat* cartoons, and the Fleischer Brothers' *Out of the Inkpot* series. A divisive pricing structure was in operation at those screenings with seats costing 3d in the stalls, but 6d in the circle.

After just fifteen months, Bernstein abandoned his experiment in specialised exhibition for children. Despite the initial excitement, attendances were low and the initiative was losing him too much money. He had counted on his experiment getting deserved support and encouragement from local communities, and particularly schools, but this had not been forthcoming. Even those who agreed that there was a need for some sort of special cinema provision for children did not agree that Bernstein had provided the solution.

For a while the baton passed from the Granada professionals to the Methodist Church. In North London, the Reverend Donald Soper organised weekly anti-immorality screenings for children. Soper believed 'cinema could be a great force for good or ill', and that contemporary commercial American cinema was, by and large, a force for ill. About 200 children sat on the floor to watch whatever wholesome film (often a silent) Soper had managed to borrow from Wardour Street that week. Sometimes Soper would decide, after a reel or two, that he had been misinformed about the film, and that it did contain immoral elements after all. In such cases the screening was abandoned and the children given their money back and sent home.

In 1934 Bernstein decided to try again with special screenings for children. He had decided that one of the reasons for his 1928–9 failure was that he had been too anxious about actively 'doing the children good'. He now thought that 'Children's shows are valuable if they satisfy the condition of providing entertainment only: they need not be educational.'

This time around he was going to pay more attention to what the children wanted (based on what they were prepared to come and see) and respond accordingly. He also abolished the distinction between stalls and circle: from now on, and for the rest of the 30s, seats were all one price – 3d – and in some cases the circle was completely closed to the Saturday morning audience.

It was the Western which proved to be the most popular kind of film with the audience, becoming the staple fare of children's cinema, not just in Bernstein's cinemas, but in the Odeons, Gaumonts and ABCs as well. Buck Jones, Tom Mix, Roy Rogers, Gene Autry, Hopalong Cassidy – these names are still redolent with meaning to the hundreds of thousands of people in this country who attended Saturday morning cinema clubs from the 30s through to the 50s. Although not made specifically for children, Westerns were widely regarded as acceptable on the grounds that they dealt with the conflict between good and evil in a ritualised and unthreatening way, with good always triumphant in the end.

The other standard ingredient introduced by Bernstein in 1934 was the American cliff-hanging serial. Several of these were Westerns, too, such as *Miracle Rider* with Tom Mix, and *Phantom Empire* starring Gene Autry. There were also a large number of crime serials, featuring cops and gangsters of various kinds; and later on the popular superheroes – Batman, Superman and Captain Marvel, and space rovers like Flash Gordon – began to appear. However, the presence of the travelogue and the newsreel in the Saturday shows suggests that the management's desire to be educational and improving was not entirely submerged by the commercially driven imperative to give the kids what they wanted.

Yet even if Granada and the other chains had found a kind of answer (albeit one that they were still having to subsidise to some extent) to the question of special provision for children, they were still reaching only about 600,000 children per week, fewer than 10 per cent of the population between the ages of five and fourteen. In general, the relationship between young people and cinema was still regarded as somewhat problematic. To address this issue, the British Film Institute convened a two-day Conference on Films for Children in November 1936. The question was formulated in a *Sight and Sound* (Autumn 1936) editorial in the following way:

the efforts which have been made until now to provide film programmes positively suitable for children have been negligible in
comparison with the number of children to be catered for, and with
the opportunities (and dangers) latent in the attendance of children
at cinemas as their main form of entertainment. . . . With increased
knowledge and realisation of the size and urgency of the problem,
it should be possible to evolve methods which might in time lead
to the provision of children's films and children's cinemas, just as
there are children's books and children's libraries.

Three hundred representatives of various organisations attended the
conference. It consisted of a screening at the Metropole Cinema in
London of a programme of films available from normal distribution
sources to an audience consisting of the representatives and 1100
school children. The programme comprised a Western, *The Eagle's
Brood*; a Laurel and Hardy comedy entitled *Sweeps*; *Bath Time at
the Zoo*; a cartoon, *The Soft Ball Game*; and a short about the making
of that cartoon.

Three papers were also presented and discussed. One was from
Sidney Bernstein, about Granada's efforts; another was from Simon
Rowson, about statistics, classification, and supply and demand; and
the third, on 'What Children Like', was presented by a psychologist,
Dr Emanuel Miller.

Bernstein, without much support from the conference, was optimis-
tic enough to echo *Sight and Sound*, expressing the hope that in time
there would be an organisation for children 'able to commission the
production of films of the type it required, just as a publisher is able
to commission an author to write a book'. Rowson confined his hopes
to more effective exploitation of the existing situation. As he put it,
'Any practical plans for providing cinema entertainment for children
must be drawn within narrow limits. Even these restricted plans can,
however, be made to serve a national good, providing healthy pleasure
for children and a by no means negligible income to the various
branches of the trade.' Only Miller had much to say about the wider
audience, concluding his address with the following assurance: 'Films
no more produce criminals than the amorality of our dreams induces
us to commit crimes. I have not known a single young delinquent, of
more than a hundred I have studied, who was deeply influenced by
films of crime. They may act the gangster, but they do not follow his
career.'

It seems unlikely everyone present at the Conference would have
agreed with Miller. Certainly at the time there were many proponents
of a rather different view on the potential harmful effects of cinema.
For example, in the Psychology and Education section of the British

Association meeting in Cambridge two years later, Dr P. B. Ballard argued that commercial films were having a mixed influence on the young. As reported in the *Daily Telegraph* of 24 August 1938, he suggested that the kind of films which had a particularly bad effect on children included those dealing with disasters, such as the sinking of a liner and the drowning of passengers; gangster films; war films and films depicting acts of adultery. In Ballard's opinion, certain bad habits, such as smoking cigarettes, were being presented in a glamorous light. He also believed that the representation of sexual relationships on the screen was a problem, declaring that 'Love-making on the screen is all too often of the baser sort. Rarely does it reveal chivalrous conduct. It is, in fact, mere lust.'

In the wake of the 1936 Conference, and criticisms such as Ballard's, the cinema chains attempted to take on board some of the chief concerns raised without alienating their audience. This occasionally generated disputes over what was appropriate material for screening to children, depending on the agendas of the parties concerned. For example, when Associated British Cinemas (ABC) programmed *The Taming of the Shrew*, starring Douglas Fairbanks and Mary Pickford, as a Saturday matinée they were criticised by both the education authorities and local cinema managers. The educationalists argued that it was not Shakespeare, and the children would be misled. The managers, on the other hand, suggested that precisely because it was Shakespeare the children would be bored. The central programmer for ABC insisted that its entertainment value was the only thing that mattered, and that the children would love it. The film was subsequently shown, apparently with success.

Likewise, the Odeon chain sought to introduce new ideas into its programming, and found them in the USSR. Since the early 30s, the Soviet cinema had addressed the issue of the value of production specifically for children. Rather than aping the simplistic, ideology-expounding puppet films of the kind being made at that time in Nazi Germany, the Soviets embarked on the production of a series of live-action fairy tales embodying universal human values. So successful were they in this aim that they were not simply dismissed in the West as Communist propaganda, and four of the films were adapted for a British audience and screened on the Odeon circuit (along with an American serial).

One of the Soviet films shown to children here was *The Little Humpback Horse* (1942), produced in Moscow by the Children's Film Studio. It tells of a decrepit Tsar who hears of a beautiful princess called Silver Morning and promises a handsome reward to anyone who can find her and bring her to him to marry. The hero Ivan, a young shepherd, is not interested in such a quest, but is eventually ordered, on pain of death, to find Silver Morning and return with her. Fortunately, he owns a little humpback horse, and together they have many adventures, before at last finding Silver Morning. However, when Ivan brings the princess to the Tsar she absolutely refuses to marry him. The humpback horse intervenes, and in the end the Tsar is out of the way, and Ivan and Silver Morning live happily ever after. The message here is that love must be earned: it cannot be bought or commanded. According to Odeon records, *The Little Humpback Horse* was popular with British children.

Another successful import from the Moscow Children's Film Studio was *The Magic Fish* (1942). When the hero, Yemelya, catches a fish, it pleads with him to be put back in the water. Yemelya agrees, and the fish rewards him by promising to grant any wish. Later, Yemelya wants to court a beautiful but bad-tempered princess. The only way to succeed is to make her laugh, and many have already failed. However, Yemelya achieves this with help from the wish-granting fish. For British children, this film was not re-voiced, but had an English commentary added, spoken by Derek McCulloch, a broadcaster who, as 'Uncle Mac', later became a doyen of the BBC radio programmes *Children's Hour* and *Children's Choice*.

The onset of war provoked a revival of the Methodist strain of thought. In 1943, J. Arthur Rank, the Methodist chairman of an emerging empire in the British Film Industry which included production and distribution companies and the Odeon and Gaumont cinema chains, enquired as to what films were being shown to the 40,000 children who at that time attended an Odeon or Gaumont every Saturday morning. As Mary Field, who later became the children's film supremo, noted:

> When he asked whether the programmes did the children good, he was disappointed to receive the negative reply that the programmes were selected as far as possible to do the children no harm but, since no entertainment films existed whose intention was to do the children good, they could not possibly be shown. Mr Rank's reply was typically Yorkshire: 'Then we will make them.'[2]

Apparently the four Soviet Films that were being shown in the Odeon clubs – *The Little Humpback Horse*, *The Magic Fish*, *The Land of Toys* and *The New Gulliver* – were considered not worth mentioning to Mr Rank. Fairy tales affirming human values were not the kind of product he had in mind. Rather, he wanted something much more explicit and didactic.

Interestingly, Rank believed that he was the first person ever to come up with the idea of the specialised production of films for children,

130

and in his announcements neither Bernstein's paper nor the Soviet experiments were ever alluded to.

There was indeed some originality in Rank's plans in that he was prepared to incorporate children's film production into the regular activity of his own commercial organisation. No state subsidy or approval or guidance was to be sought, Rank was going to pay for this production programme himself. This new initiative entailed some rather grandiloquent statements on Rank's part. Two years after decreeing the production of films that would 'do children good', he was defending himself in an interview thus:

> I have heard it said that grave danger exists in the work I am trying to do – as a private individual might – with the highest motives. It has been said that I may affect, in the execution of my plans, the whole range of thought of the nation's young people. I appreciate fully the sincerity of those fears. I maintain nevertheless that what I am striving to achieve is the improvement of a child's outlook on life during its most receptive period, without relation to any particular political or religious creed. Our one concern is to assist them to grow into better men or women.[3]

The first fruit of Rank's desire to 'do them good' was a ten-minute film made under wartime conditions in the foggy October of 1943. In the making of this film two key moments occurred. The first was at script stage. Originally titled *The Bicycle*, the project emerged from within a department called Gaumont-British Instructional Films, with advice on the writing of the script coming from cinema club controllers (to whose hands-on expertise Rank was prepared to defer in matters of detail). The educational purpose of the film was to wean children away from the folk wisdom of the idea, 'finders, keepers', and demonstrate that finding can actually constitute stealing in the eyes of the law. At the initial script stage, *The Bicycle* consisted mainly of a lesson in moral instruction, alleviated very little by way of action. The director was not happy with the script, and after discussions it was decided that G-B Instructional would seek permission from the club controllers to rewrite the story to include a chase sequence. This was acceptable to the controllers, provided it didn't impede the film's message, and justified the changing of the title from *The Bicycle* to *Tom's Ride*.

The other key moment occurred after the film had been made. There had been no agreement on how it was to end, so three possible endings were filmed. The story concerns a boy named Tom who finds a wallet with five pounds in it – enough to buy the bicycle that he desperately wants. He is persuaded by his older sister not to spend the money, since that would be a kind of stealing. Tom then discovers the name and address of the owner of the wallet, and pursues her, on his sister's bicycle, to the railway station, where the woman, unaware that she has no money, is planning to travel to London to see her son invested by the King. Problems such as level-crossing gates hinder Tom's progress, but he gets to the station platform and returns the money just in time for the woman to catch her train.

After viewing the film up to this point, Rank and his executives found themselves locked in argument over whether or not Tom should get a material reward for his honesty and his heroic effort. In a Russian fairy story he would certainly have got something mysterious or magical, perhaps. However, Rank decided that virtue must be presented as its own reward. Tom would get the satisfaction of linking into the war effort, and of knowing that he had saved a woman from missing the most important engagement of her life – but nothing else. Later, after *Tom's Ride* had been screened in the Odeon and Gaumont clubs, the controllers reported that many of the children were disappointed that Tom did not receive a reward. Perhaps these children had been influenced by films like *The Magic Fish*.

In any case, *Tom's Ride* was to mark the beginning of a line of film specialist production which is now almost fifty years old. Rank followed up *Tom's Ride* with a two-reel school story called *Sports Day* in 1944, produced this time by a new unit called Children's Entertainment Films (CEF), headed by Mary Field. *Sports Day* was not without its own controversies. The moral point of the film was meant to be an injunction against cruelty to animals. The central incident which illustrated the theme involved some children tying a tin can to a dog's tail. However, the CEF's project of doing children good clashed with the British Board of Film Censors' project of doing animals good. The Board's insistence then, as now, is that animals must never be seen to be suffering just to suit the purposes of a fiction. Consequently, the BBFC were not prepared to give the film a certificate of any kind unless the tin can episode was cut. This was an extreme example of a general problem which the CEF had to grapple with: how to show good overcoming evil, without showing the evil.

Problems also arose over the 1946 three-reeler, *Jean's Plan*, the CEF's longest film to date. It was set against a background of English canals and featured the 16-year-old Jean Simmons in the central role. The film's fairly obtrusive moral point was made when the greedy villain was made, at the end, to look ridiculous. More importantly, it had a chase sequence. *Tom's Ride* had proved that children like chases, so *Jean's Plan* gave them a long and exciting one. However, it turned out to be too exciting for the BBFC, who gave the film an 'A' Certificate. The problem for the Board was that, during the chase, children were shown as being frightened and these shots would have to be cut out before the film could be awarded the desired 'U' certificate. As a result, the CEF accepted, and came to regard as wise, the BBFC's dictum that they must never show a frightened child on the screen, because, as Mary Field put it: 'A young audience tends to associate itself with the children in the film and, so long as they are not visibly frightened, the audience is not frightened either.'

One consequence of the emergence of these guidelines as to what constituted suitable cinema for children was the opening up of a rift between the Odeon cinema chain and the hitherto popular fairy tale films from the Soviet Union. Even in 1952, Mary Field was claiming that she admired Soviet films and had been much influenced by them. In her view, these productions, though different in style and technique, had exactly the same purpose as the British films came to have: 'to provide first-class entertainment while at the same time introducing, as a background to the story, the kind of conduct that is universally admired – patience, hard work, collaboration, kindness and good temper'. But traffic had always been entirely one way, with the USSR never reciprocating by importing a single CEF film. Moreover, things were changing at home in that the CEF productions had established social realism as the preferred house style, with the result that fantasy was no longer the favoured aesthetic in the realm of children's cinema.

One Soviet film that might have seemed to have everything going for it was *The Magic Seed*, produced in 1945 by Sergei Eisenstein. It told the story of Andreyka and Maryka and their quest for the seed of happiness. In order to get it, they must find and fight the wicked ogre Karamur, who keeps it locked up in his cellar, because without it he will die. Eventually Andreyka and Maryka, with the help of a magic flute, a blacksmith, a scientist, and a young black slave, defeat Karamur and set out to spread happiness everywhere.

The Magic Seed obviously had much to commend it to Mary Field and the post-war Western world. It had Eisenstein's name associated with it, it featured gender equality and interracial co-operation, it had the triumph of good over totalitarian evil, and it did not explicitly identify Communism as the magic seed. But it also contained what the *Monthly Film Bulletin* of January 1945 referred to as 'scenes that would be terrifying for very young children', and which Field described as 'long sequences showing monsters with horrible hands and faces'.

Although the BBFC objected to frightened children on the screen, it didn't object to frightened children in the seats, and gave *The Magic Seed* a 'U' certificate. In so doing it possibly recalled the barrage of criticism which had, ten years earlier, greeted its award of an 'A' certificate to Disney's *Snow White and the Seven Dwarfs*, on the grounds that the witch was too frightening for a child to encounter without a parent. They subsequently changed the certificate to a 'U'. The Board were now invoking the concept of the 'healthy fright' in the case of *The Magic Seed*. This did not sway Mary Field who insisted that the film was not suitable for children, made no attempt to negotiate an edited version, and subsequently dropped it, along with *The Stone Flower* (1947) – another Soviet film of which many people outside the CEF thought highly.

In fact, during the entire existence of the CEF from 1943 to 1950, only one film from the Moscow Studios was taken up and shown in the Odeon Saturday cinema clubs. This was *The Elephant and the Skipping Rope* (1945), a half-hour lesson in unselfishness couched in the form of a story about a girl who wants to be a champion skipper. In a dream an elephant tells her that she must perform a good deed for someone before she can ever become a champion. When she finally finds someone who really needs her help, the only way she can give it is by sacrificing her precious rope. After that she has skill enough to lead all the other skippers. This film was popular with Saturday morning audiences, especially the younger members, but Mary Field none the less refered to it disparagingly as 'approximating more closely to the adult conception of a film for children than our own product does'.

This 'own product' was indeed at that time enjoying remarkable popularity among children and adults, both at home and abroad. CEF's interpretation of Rank's idea of 'doing them good' had moved on from the overt moralising of *Tom's Ride* to simply offering attractive examples of thoughtful, tolerant, responsible behaviour. Indeed, the sermonising was now more prevalent in front of the screen than on it, as Odeon cinema managers tried each week to lead the children in a recitation of the Club promise, a series of pledges ending: 'I promise to try and make this great country of ours a better place to live in.'

The CEF were always very conscious that they were operating in a free-market context: if the children didn't fancy what was on offer at an Odeon, they could take their sixpence elsewhere – probably to an ABC cinema. Mary Field despised the ABC chain, believing them to be cynical and opportunistic. She wrote:

> The aim of the Rank Group was gradually to accustom children to specially made story films that were 'good' for them; our rivals' aim was to excite and amuse the children for the passing moment by means of any adult film that had enough action to catch their visual attention.

But she knew that the children themselves did not make such a distinction.

The CEF had studied audience response, not only through managers' reports but also by way of the use of infra-red photography. Across the UK, and in the Dominions, photographs of the audience had been taken during the course of screenings, without the children being aware this was happening; these photographs were then matched up with stills showing the action on the screen at that moment. From their overall findings the CEF had developed a set of production maxims by which they hoped to satisfy both the children and Rank. In essence, some of these maxims were:

- There is no need for violence on the screen, but there must be plenty of activity.
- Girls must be given fair representation, and should not always be shown in 'feminine' roles.
- Our audiences prefer to see the main parts played by ordinary children like themselves, and not by the sweet little girls and waif-like little boys that enthral adult filmgoers.
- Film viewing is a two-way affair, and the pleasure in a picture depends very largely on what the audience contributes to its own entertainment.

The best-known example of the kind of film produced within this context is *Bush Christmas* (1946). Filmed in Australia, it tells the story of five children alone in the bush on the trail of two horse thieves. The children's ages range from six to twelve (that of CEF's target audience). One of the children is a fairly strong and spirited girl. One of the boys is black, and he too is resourceful; another wears glasses. Working together, the children track the thieves without being spotted. At night, out in the bush, they reclaim the horses and remove the thieves' boots. Later they are captured by the thieves and suspended on meat-hooks, but even that does not scare them.

Bush Christmas unquestionably provoked wild enthusiasm among children who saw it. Cinema managers requested it again and again, and adults who saw it as children in the 40s still remember it affectionately and vividly. Mary Field referred to it proudly as 'having introduced the racial problem indirectly' and as being 'considered, in most countries where it has been shown, as the ideal children's film'. Forty years after being made, when I saw it in Munich with a crowd of German children, it was still capable of creating for all of us an atmosphere of shared fun and excitement. *Bush Christmas* was arguably the CEF's finest hour.

Children's Entertainment Films survived until 1950, endlessly

Bush Christmas (Ralph Smart, 1947)

experimenting, and seeking to refine its techniques. It produced serials, nature films, a ballet film, a circus film, magazine films, 'Let's Sing Together' films, animation – even the occasional fantasy. It imported and adapted children's films from Sweden and Czechoslovakia. It even re-edited material meant for adults – for example, making *Tale of a Trawler* out of a longer documentary on cod-fishing in the North Sea.

But this had all cost money, and by 1950 Rank felt that he had made his point about the need for specialised children's cinema. After the press launch of CEF in 1944 he had been reported as saying: 'Incidentally, if young people get the habit of cinema-going, we shall probably make a profit out of them in six or seven years' time.' Six years on and Rank, like most of the British film industry at the time, was experiencing financial hardship and, as it had not ultimately proved to be the profitable venture he had predicted, the CEF was closed down.

How successful had Rank been in 'doing them good'? Had he 'affected the entire range of thought of the nation's young people' or 'assisted them to grow into better men and women', as he suggested he would? There is no doubt that the majority of the nation's young people were completely unaffected by Rank's initiative, for the simple reason that they never went to a Saturday matinée cinema club, and therefore never saw a CEF production, or recited the Club Promise. There was a town and country divide in that the Clubs were situated

136

in urban areas. More importantly, there was a class divide, with the overwhelming majority of children who attended Saturday cinema clubs coming from working-class families. By and large, teachers, MPs and middle-class parents continued to distrust the matinées, calling them 'pernicious' in letters to the press. They made no distinction between the Odeon clubs and other exhibitors, despite Rank's well-publicised good intentions. Indeed, these intentions were often dismissed with comments like: 'The only person to benefit from Mr Rank's thoughtfulness for children is Mr Rank himself.' A letter to *The Housewife*, in September 1946, demonstrates the typical attitudes of the middle classes:

> For a long time my boy craved to go to Saturday matinées, and I finally let him, on the principle that the sooner he went, the sooner it would pass out of his system. After six weeks he gave it up as boring (perhaps because he had to pay for it out of his own money!). Then he discovered that free film shows were being given each fortnight at the local library. The first evening he went, he was turned away, as children under sixteen had to be with an adult. So I was dragged in as an entrance fee. And now I would not miss these winter shows either! They consist of shorts, and sometimes a Disney cartoon. But there is always a theme to connect them, and a local celebrity to lecture on the topic. In this way, we have learned about town planning, money, health, child welfare, education and farming. . . . And the chats afterwards on the way home in the dark with the children were a fine finish to a good evening.

The letter-writer does not indicate what cinema chain her son went to for six weeks: they were all the same to her. It was not that the middle classes did not want their children 'improved'; they just could not accept that a large auditorium, on a Saturday morning, with hundreds of other children and very few adults, was a place where such improvement could happen.

Another important factor reducing the possible effectiveness of the 'do-good' policy was that most children who went to the cinema not only shopped around on Saturday mornings if they had more than one club to choose from, but they also went to the cinema at other times of the week – sometimes with their family, sometimes with friends, sometimes alone. Some Odeon club children who were questioned in 1947 talked about seeing 'A' certificate films such as *Odd Man Out* (James Mason as an IRA killer on the run), *Black Narcissus* (Powell and Presburger's study of repressed sexuality among nuns in the Himalayas) and *Fighting Lady* (a war film set in the Philippines) in the same breath that they talked about the CEF's *Bush Christmas* and Ealing's boys-and-crooks film *Hue and Cry*. The cinema was a place for fun and excitement, and if that was on offer, then it did not matter what time of day it was, or what day of the week it was.

A final limiting aspect of the operation was that there were far more Saturdays than there were specially made films. There was no way that CEF could quickly make or find enough of the right kind of films to fill two hours every Saturday continuously. It had been calculated that within three years there would be a more or less complete turnover of membership in a Saturday cinema club. Therefore, after screening 156 programmes, a club would be able to go back to the beginning and start again, confident that all those who had seen it before would have either left or forgotten it. However, at no stage did CEF come anywhere near to having 156 hand-picked programmes, so there were always all sorts of other films from various sources, such as Westerns, a Disney cartoon or a cliff-hanger serial.

It seems it was these last two kinds of films which, except for the occasional CEF production like *Bush Christmas*, had the most impact on children. Before the war, Rank clubs had been called, significantly, Mickey Mouse Clubs. That name had been discontinued, but it would still have been appropriate. The CEF and the rest of the cinema club movement were well aware of the power and popularity of Mickey Mouse. In fact, if Disney had allowed his feature films to be shown in Saturday matinées, then the CEF would have felt that it had less of a mountain to climb. But the Walt Disney Company have always insisted that their films are not children's films but are, rather, made for 'the child in all of us', and therefore are available only for mixed audiences. It is a policy which has certainly done Disney good!

The cliff-hanger serial was an even stronger common bond among cinema club members. It did not matter what club you were a member of, the only important question seems to have been: which serials did you see? For people who experienced agonies of suspense every week for fifteen weeks, while the plot unwound its tortuous length, the memories remain strong. However, in the end, it was probably the collectivity of the shared experience, rather than the themes of the films themselves, which had the more lasting influence on Saturday morning cinema goers.

Within a year of its demise the CEF was replaced by the Children's Film Foundation, a pan-industry body financed by the Eady Levy, a tax on the price of cinema seats. Eady money was administered by a film industry committee, and could only be used for cinema-related purposes. Gone was the old distinction between the Odeons and the rest. Odeons, ABCs and independents all had equal shares in the forthcoming production of the CFF. The new body did not exactly take over from the CEF the requirement to 'do them good'. However,

Mary Field was once again at the helm, and the Foundation's constitution still lists among its objects: 'To demonstrate to educationalists and social workers that the film industry in this country aims at producing and exhibiting films which are suitable in every way for children.' The Foundation still exists; and its history is yet to be written.

Notes

1. This and subsequent Bernstein quotations are taken from an article in *Sight and Sound*, Winter 1936.
2. This and subsequent quotations attributed to Mary Field are taken from her book, *Good Company: The Story of Children's Entertainment Film Movement in Great Britain, 1943–50* (London: Longman's, 1952).
3. From *Motion Picture Herald*, January 1946.

ERRATA

New Questions of British Cinema

BFI Working Papers, 1992

There were a number of factual errors in Stephen Romer's account of *Distant Voices, Still Lives* in his contribution 'Production Strategies in the UK'. Rather than correct the errors one by one, it is easier to set out the history of the project from my perspective as Head of Production at the BFI during that period.

After the completion of *Distant Voices*, I felt very strongly that if we released a 45-minute film it would find only a small audience. I talked this over with Terence Davies and he told me he had always envisaged a second film, of roughly equal length. I persuaded him that it was worth holding on to *Distant Voices* while he wrote, and I tried to raise the finance for, the second part. This decision was enthusiastically supported by my Production Board. I then arranged a screening of *Distant Voices* for Jeremy Isaacs and David Rose. They immediately agreed to put £200,000 into the second half. By the time the script was complete and the budget had been drawn up, it was clear that *Still Lives* was going to cost £350,000. The Board agreed to allocate a further £100,000 and Eckhart Stein of ZDF provided the final £50,000 to allow us to go into production.

Colin MacCabe
Head of Media, Education and Research
British Film Institute
May 1993